Violence

Library of Congress Cataloging-in-Publication Data

Fava, Giuseppe.
[Violenza. English]
Violence : a Sicilian drama in three acts / Giuseppe Fava ; translated into English by Gaetano Cipolla.
p. cm.
ISBN 1-881901-46-7 (pbk.)
I. Cipolla, Gaetano, 1937- II. Title.
PQ4866.A88V513 2007
852'.914—dc22
2007011698

Printed and bound in Canada

Acknowledgments

The publisher gratefully acknowledges receipt of a grant from Arba Sicula which made in part the publication of this volume possible.

This is a translation of the play *La Violenza*, originally published in Catania by Tringale Editore in 1988.

The publisher is grateful to Nicolo D'Alessandro for the use of his China ink drawing of "La Giustizia" for the cover.

For information and for orders, write to:
LEGAS

P.O. Box 149
Mineola, New York
11501 – USA
Fax (718) 990 – 5954

3 Wood Aster Bay
Ottawa, Ontario
K2 1D3 Canada
Fax (613.) 562-5138

www.legaspublishing.com

Giuseppe Fava

Violence

A Sicilian Drama in Three Acts

Preface

by Brendan N. Ward

Translated into English by

Gaetano Cipolla

LEGAS

Table of Contents

Preface by Brendan Ward 7

List of Characters in Order of Appearance 12

Act I 13

Act II 53

Act III 95

PREFACE

Giuseppe Fava, one of the foremost Italian journalists who opposed the Sicilian Mafia, was a writer, essayist, journalist, playwright, screenwriter, and well known painter.

Fava was born in Palazzo Acreide, in the Sicilian province of Siracusa, September 15, 1925. He died a violent death 59 years later, the evening of January 5, 1984, when a mafia gunman shot him dead with 5- 7.65 mm bullets to the head. The assassination took place in Catania, the city he so loved, on Via dello Stadio, the street just next door to the Verga Theater, where so many of his major plays had their premiere. The street is now named after him.

Fava studied at the *liceo classico* in Siracusa until he moved to Catania to study Law. He took his law degree in 1947 and began to practice. But his literary vocation, which had emerged at the Liceo in Siracusa, would not stay dormant. He turned increasingly to journalism. In the early 50's, he worked as a writer first for Nello Simili's *Giornale dell'isola*, then at the *Corriere di Sicilia*, and later at *Le Ultimissime* and at the magazines *Tempo Illustrato* and *Domenica del Corriere*, where, as correspondent, he wrote about Sicilian affairs, current events, and the Cinema.

During the years after 1956 he began his intense collaboration as writer and reporter for *La Sicilia* and remained affiliated with it for most of his professional life. It is here where he first made his mark as a social critic and cultural commentator. He became head reporter of Catania's daily newspaper, *Espresso Sera*, in 1956, then under the leadership of Girolamo Damigella. He remained there until 1978. It is during this period that Fava used his considerable literary prowess to deeply explore the passion and the drama of his native Sicily, its remarkable people, and its unique troubles. His literary work as journalist, playwright and later as novelist, intensified during these years and he achieved fame for the brilliance of his style and for the incisiveness of his observations.

In 1967 he published *Processo alla Sicilia* in Palermo. It is a collection of important journalism first published by him in *La Sicilia*. It engulfed Fava in controversy and brought him considerable notoriety. A volume of short stories, *Pagine*, is published shortly afterwards, at Catania, in 1969.

His first play, *Cronaca di un uomo* is produced in 1966. It wins the Premio Vallecorsi. In 1970 his play *La Violenza* is produced at the Verga Theater in Catania. It wins the Premio IDI and is adapted into the film *Violenza quinto potere*, directed by Florestano Vancini. Other plays follow: *Il proboviro*. 1972; *Bello bellissimo*, 1974. *Opera buffa*, 1979. etc. All of Fava's plays are collected in three hefty volumes published after his death: Giuseppe Fava: *Teatro*, Catania. 1988.

His novel *Gente di rispetto* (Bompiani, 1975), a story of Sicilian life told with great urgency and impact, brings Fava national attention. The novel is later adapted into a powerful film, directed by Luigi Zampa.

Two more novels followed: *Prima che vi uccidano* (Bompiani, 1977, but written in the 60's, and *Passione di Michele* (Cappelli, 1980) based on his own screenplay for the film "Palermo oder Wolfsburg" directed by Werner Schroter, which took the Golden Bear Award at the Berlin Film Festival in 1980.

I Siciliani, another collection of journalistic investigations appears in 1978. It consolidated Fava's reputation as an astute social critic and moral champion and as a leftist intellectual. His notoriety was consolidated also as a result of his regular radio broadcasts (*Voi ed io*, for RAI's first channel) which won him a great many admirers but also some very powerful enemies. The danger of his advocacy for social justice and the effect it was having on the population of Catania was apparent to the leaders of the new Mafia, then infiltrating into all levels of "correct" society: the police, the judicial establishment, and, especially, business enterprise. Another radio champion of social justice would pay with his life for such advocacy—the subject of the recent film *I cento passi* directed by Marco Tullio Giordano. In June of 1980 Fava becomes director of the important daily *Il Giornale del Sud*, a newspaper sustained by a group of politicians and businessmen from Catania. Fava sees a chance to combine journalistic integrity with humanitarian activism. He assembles a brilliant team of young writers, selected, mostly, from socially conscious activists who hold Fava up as their moral teacher.

The group includes Fava's son, Claudio, (now a member of the EU Parliament) and other young activists such as Riccardo Orioles, Michele Gambino. Antonio Roccuzzo, Rosario Lanza and Elena Brancati. The Fava group decides to focus on problems inextricably linked to poorly understood changes in the socio-economic stratum of Sicily, changes which have created a new breed of powerful men in Catania, men involved in an unholy alliance combining politics, financial interests and organized crime. The Fava group defy caution and start investigating this new Mafia. this hidden power emerging in Catania. They track down its members, expose their workings, and reveal their corrupt practices in the newspaper for all to see.

As Fava will explain later in *I Siciliani*: "The moral climate of society is this: power has isolated itself from everything. It has placed itself in a dimension in which everything that happens outside of itself, in the real nation, does not affect it at all. Nothing offends this Power: neither accusations, nor denunciations, not pain, not desperation, not revolt. This Power resides in its own special place. Newspapers, the theatre, the cinema—they all pass along without hurting it. Politicians, businessmen, judges—they all stand up and applaud it…for this Power is convinced of its own invulnerability." ("I Quattro cavalieri dell'apocalisse mafiosa", published in the first issue of "I Siciliani", n.1. January, 1983.)

The origins of the new Mafia of Fava's investigations can be traced to this time, in the early 80's when, in Catania, the extension of the Mafia's power coincided with a crisis in the local legal authority and also a crisis in the local political hierarchy. The resulting power vacuum allowed organized crime to infiltrate the Catania social structure. As Chief Officer C. A. Dalla Chiesa explained in the famous interview he gave to G. Bocca (*La Repubblica*, August 8, 1982): the "historic turning point" in the evolution of the new Mafia was the opening in Palermo of 4 major real-estate ventures organized in Catania by the Catania Mafia.

There was nothing "petty crime" about the Catania real-estate venture in Palermo. Something new was indeed happening in Catania and Fava had recognized it. The Mafia had become "professionalized" and were now thoroughly "middle class," hardly distinguishable from other members of the professional classes.

As he said in his final interview with Enzo Biagi, broadcast on *Retequattro*, December 28, 1983—7 days before his assassination: "Mafiosi are in parliament, sometimes they are ministers, sometimes bankers. Mafiosi are those who are in charge of the nation right now. You cannot define "mafioso" as a small time crook who forces you to pay a cut of your small business. This is small stuff that exists in all Italian cities, in all European cities. The problem of the Mafia is much greater, much more tragic."

Fava's unrestrained style of reporting in *Il Giornale del Sud* and the muckraking stirrings of his journalist group made him fierce enemies and these fierce enemies resolved to silence him and his investigative team of youngsters. Fava is forced out of his Editor position at *Il Giornale del Sud*. Later inquiries reveal that the two men who fired Fava, Salvatore Lo Turco and Gaetano Graci, are, in fact, close associates of the Mafia boss, Nitto Santapaola. The public reason given for Fava's firing is his editorial support for the campaign to ban the presence of nuclear warheads at the NATO military base in Comiso. Fava responds to his attackers by intensifying his social activism. He establishes the Radar Co-Op, based in Sant'Agata Li Battiati, and staffs it with his young journalists from *Giornale del Sud*. In 1982. Fava buys two bicolor offset 70/100 machines and begins publishing the monthly *I Siciliani*, an organ to provide news and commentary to the entire Island of Sicily and to all of Italy's south. He will use the monthly *I Siciliani* to proclaim his intense revulsion of the new Mafia. The first issue appears on January 1, 1983 and launches his attack: "*I Siciliani* is born at a time when the problem of the South has finally become, historically speaking, the problem of the entire country. *I Siciliani* aims to be the critical document of all Southern reality, which, for better or for worse, belongs to all the Italian people." *I Siciliani* becomes one of the defining moments in the anti-mafia movement. *I Siciliani* will be a monthly newspaper but also a book to circulate. A book "of the history we live, written day by day." His article for the first issue— "The Four Horsemen of the Mafia Apocalypse"—becomes a publishing sensation launching the monthly brilliantly. Fava's voice will not be silenced despite all the New Mafia's efforts.

Fava's passion for truth, which drives him deeper and deeper into danger at *I Siciliani* is already evident in his famous interview for *La Sicilia* of January 25, 1975: "Journalism cannot just be the search for news…it is the search for truth in everything involving society, the citizen, man himself…(it is) a continuous civil aggression on reality, first to discover the news (particularly that which is not obvious, that which is hidden) and then to distil these discoveries into something that is absolutely truthful, and, finally, to interpret it." *I Siciliani* becomes indeed "a continuous aggression on reality".

The monthly stridently attacks political and entrepreneurial loyalties, showing how politicians and businessmen owe their positions to the power of the new Mafia. *I Siciliani* tries mightily to wake up society, to make a reticent public come to grips with the magnitude of the Mafia's spreading malignancy.

But the fight for real authority in Catania, political, legal and economic authority, was already won by the new Mafia. They decide it is time to stop Fava. His was a single denunciatory voice, exposing them to public scrutiny. Muting that voice will send a clear signal to anyone thinking of obstructing their progress and future proceedings.

The night of January 5, 1984, Fava is ambushed and shot dead in front of his own theatre. The murderer is not identified. Indeed the investigation gets seriously thrown off-track and drags on endlessly until it nearly gets forgotten as just one more unsolved Sicilian crime. It is only after numerous more murders. including the car-bomb death of the great Italian jurist, Giovanni Falcone, and the blatant kidnapping and murder of the former Italian Prime Minister, Aldo Moro, that, finally the Mafia in Sicily is brought to some justice.

In the famous trial called "Orsa Maggiore 3" of 1998, the Mafia boss

Nitto Santapaola, is convicted of ordering the killings of Giuseppe Fava and police inspector Giovanni Lizzo. Santapaola is sentenced to life imprisonment. Marcello D'Agata and Francesco Giammuso are convicted of organizing the killing. Aldo Ercolano and Maurizio Avola are identified as the executioners. Ercolano gets life imprisonment but Avola, who turned state's evidence, and collaborated with the police, identifying numerous other Mafiosi, is sentenced to six years and six months. In 2001, Santapaola's and Ercolano's life sentences are confirmed by the Appeals Court of Catania. The sentences of Marcello D'Agata and Francesco Giammuso, the organizers of the murder, are absolved. Giuseppe Fava, author, painter, inspirer of the young, a man of multiple interests, a socialist with ideals but no party affiliation, emotionally tied to a Verghian and earthly conception of Sicily, who all his life and in all his works promoted a message of liberation and hope for the oppressed and for those who suffer, died, finally, because he believed in the undying perfectibility of man. At the heart of his work was a call to reformation, a petition to the heart and soul, where, he firmly believed, the goodness of the Sicilian people lay. He loved Sicily fiercely and he loved Catania even more fiercely. Of his city, whose faults he knew better than perhaps any other man of his time, he wrote passionately in terms of his complex feelings for her, feelings that came close to a forbidden love.

His relationship with Catania, he writes, "are those of a precise, sentimental rapport. The same as one might have by falling desperately in love with a whore. You can't do anything about it. You know she's a whore. She's vulgar, dirty, a betrayer. She let's herself be bought by anybody with money. She's obscene, a liar, bossy, but she is also jovial, happy, even violently so. She knows all the tricks and all the vices of love, and lets you taste them all. Then, she immediately runs away with another man." (Giuseppe Fava, *I Siciliani*, Cappelli, 1980).

Brendan N. Ward
Professor
The School of the Arts,
Columbia University, New York.

List of Characters in Order of Appearance

Rosalia Alicata
Prosecutor
Defense Attorney
Anna Laurini-Congelin, widow
Defendant Luciano Verzì
Defendant Emanuele Crupi
Defendant Amedeo Barresi
Adriana Miceli, a prostitute
Antonio Golino, Police Sergeant
Defendant Filippo Giacalone
Defendant Antonino Gagliano
Defendant Giacomo Colosi
Congressman Mario Zaccaria
Professor Luciano Salemi
Witness I
Witness II
Witness III
Salvatore Licitra, a boy
Defendant Rosario Vacirca
Virna Florena, Widow
Carabiniere
and Other Defendants
Rosalia Savoca

Act I

(A dark stage. A woman sits in the back bathed in a yellowish light, like a beam descending from a church nave. Suddenly a flash shines a light on that unmoving human figure and a large photo of her face close-up is projected onto the wall – she is old, worn-out, grim, with long hair. Her features are immobile and desperate. A guitar softly plays a few chords of a very sad tune.)

THE WOMAN – My name is Rosalia Savoca. I am Venero Alicata's mother. My son was ambushed the night of October 18. You cannot imagine the man my son was, his courage ...that's why they murdered him... His killer is now in this room... I want to see him buried alive in a tomb. I want to know every day that he's suffering, wants to see his children, but can't...that he's ill and dying...

(The image fades and the stage light comes on at the same time. The stage is a courtroom seen from the judges' perspective. The atmosphere is bare, full of shadows, suggesting perhaps an old desecrated church. On the left side, in the darkest part of the room, there is a nearly diagonal platform, a double row of benches where the defendants sit, the farthest of which remain enveloped in shadows at the back of the room. Next to the platform, in the foreground, the Prosecutor's bench. In the background, a bare gray wall, against which the woman dressed in black, sits quietly on a bench.)

A LOUD VOICE – The Jury!

(Everyone stands and remains standing for a few seconds, silently looking toward the front. The only one who remains standing is the Prosecutor who approaches the audience as though it were the Jury. All the others are seated quietly in the poorly lit room.)

PROSECUTOR – Gentlemen of the Jury, the deeds you will be called to judge are a tragedy in which you personally involved every day. In this room, we can ask you for an act of justice only for the men who were murdered, but the tragedy is greater and more terrible. It touches not only the lives of a few citizens, but every human relationship, indeed, the very freedom of human beings... All you will hear me relate took place in the last two years – sixteen murders committed with unheard-of cruelty. I will tell you the basic facts, in chronological order, so you can understand them and render judgment –

(At the same time, the picture of a man lying on the street is projected onto the back wall. His arms are wide open, his white shirt soaked in blood. There is a line of blood on his face. From this point forward for every murder related by the Prosecutor the victim's

photo will be projected onto the back wall. The photos should be like those printed in newspapers articles.)

On the night of October 18, union organizer Venero Alicata and Mario Scibilia, an 8-year-old boy, were gunned down in a deserted street. Venero Alicata was hit with three bullets in the chest and one in the back of the neck, and Mario Scibilia, who was playing by a window in his house, was killed instantly by a single bullet in his right eye.

Two months later, middlemen Francesco Farina and Pietro Garofalo shot at the outskirts of town as they were returning home on a motorcycle. The murderers, probably two, opened fire with automatic weapons hitting the victims with at least fifty bullets on various parts of their bodies.

Barely fifteen days later, on a street of the same suburbs, ex-con Gaetano Nascimbene was struck with two shotgun blasts. The murderer finished him with three pistol shots to the back of the head and stuck a rock in his mouth as a sign of contempt.

The sixth murder took place in the heart of town at nine P.M. A single shotgun blast, point blank, that nearly decapitated Carmelo Licitra, a 36-year old mechanic. The body remained stretched out in the middle of the street more than an hour before anyone dared to come out of their homes to try to succor him…

The seventh victim was probably the only one who recognized his murderers. His name was Giovanni Savoca, a huge, bald man of seventy, who was returning home on his bike. When he saw the men waiting for him in a car, he steered his bike down a hilly street, but a hail of lead smashed one of his arms, another blast made a hole in his back, and he, though already dead, amazingly continued to ride his bike all the way to the bottom of the hill, where he crashed. This murder too showed the killers' contempt. The shotgun was loaded with lead pellets mixed with bits of metal and nails. His body had ninety-two holes…

The eighth murder seemed the most inexplicable and gravest of all– on the night of March 18, on a deserted city street, Police Commissioner Ettore Florena was killed as he was walking home with his wife. Six bullets fired point blank hit him in the chest, throat and head, killing him instantly…

The other eight murders were really a massacre. An explosion, a big flash! The police had been called to check an abandoned car, an Alfa Romeo Giulietta, for explosives. The bomb squad specialists cut all the wires, opened all the doors, removed the wheels and even parts of the motor. Only the trunk remained unopened and the task to open it fell to a 24 year-old police lieutenant. Death was waiting inside that trunk–the blast reached 150 feet into the air, demolishing every building around. The remains of the eight policemen were dispersed in the crater of the explosion. They found only a pistol, a finger with a wedding ring, two rank tabs from a uniform, two officer's stars and an officer's cap....

...The men responsible for these sixteen murders, and perhaps for fifty others, at least, for whom we cannot charge them because the bodies have vanished without leaving a trace, are inside that cage...

(*He sits down slowly.*)

Before beginning their interrogation we need to proceed with a brief preliminary formality. Almost all the victims' relatives refused to press charges. One who had agreed to press charges against the defendants, the mother of Officer Eugenio Congelin, told me she intends to withdraw her charges. We must therefore proceed with a preliminary interrogation...

(*He calls out.*)

Anna Laurini!

(*The mother of the policeman appears from the back on the left. A sixty-year old woman, dressed in black. She comes forward and stops to face the Court. Her eyes are darting about restlessly.*)

PROSECUTOR – Please tell the Court your first and last name.

WOMAN – Anna Laurini-Congelin, widow.

PROSECUTOR – What was your relationship with Officer Eugenio Congelin?

WOMAN – (*In a very low voice.*) I am his mother!

PROSECUTOR – Mrs. Congelin, is it true you no longer want to be a plaintiff in this case?

WOMAN – (*Nodding briefly.*) Yes, Sir!

PROSECUTOR – Madam, before you leave, can you tell the Court how you learned that your son had been killed...?

(*As the woman does not answer, he gently calls her attention.*)

Madam...

WOMAN – I received a telegram.

PROSECUTOR – What was written in the telegram?

WOMAN – Ministry of Defense–Officer Eugenio Congelin, fallen in the line of duty.

PROSECUTOR – Nothing else?

WOMAN – No, Sir.

PROSECUTOR – At this point, Madam you did not know how your son had died. How did they communicate with you?

WOMAN – I received a yellow envelope with a letter signed by the General and another smaller yellow envelope.

PROSECUTOR – What did the smaller envelope contain?

(*The woman does not answer, looking straight ahead without moving. Then she closes her eyes.*)

Madam, would you please tell us what was inside the smaller envelope?

WOMAN – A gold ring and a policeman's star.

PROSECUTOR – Wasn't there a letter, a sheet of paper…?

WOMAN – Yes, Sir. A sheet of paper…

PROSECUTOR – What was written on that sheet?

WOMAN – We are sending you all we were able to find of Officer Eugenio Congelin at the site of the explosion.

PROSECUTOR – Madam, I must ask you a very important question. You have refused to press charges against the defendants. Can you explain why?

(*The woman does not answer.*)

PROSECUTOR – Madam, in that cage there are men accused of your son's murder, yet you refused to press charges. Why?

(*The woman still refuses to answer, remaining motionless.*)

PROSECUTOR – (*Screaming.*) Look into my eyes, Madam. Some of those men killed your son, they destroyed him, tore him to pieces. Eugenio Congelin was your son, Madam, barely twenty-two years old. He was torn to pieces in a second, and all he represented on the face of this earth was sent to you in a yellow envelope. Yet, you refuse to accuse the killers. Didn't you have any money to pay for a lawyer, Madam?

(*The woman remains motionless, without a sound.*)

PROSECUTOR – Have you other children, Madam? Are you afraid for them?

(*The woman continues to stare into space silently.*)

PROSECUTOR – You may go…

(*The woman does not even try any gestures of leave-taking, and proceeds toward the exit at the back of the stage. Almost at the same time the defense attorney rises and addresses the Court. He speaks calmly holding a dossier that he occasionally places on the table and picks up again.)*

DEFENSE ATTORNEY – With the Prosecutor's permission, before cross-examining defendants and witnesses, I formally request that the Court order a psychiatric evaluation of Rosario Vacirca on whose testimony much of the prosecution's case rests... At this time, to make it possible for the Court to judge with absolute objectivity, I need to make a few remarks. I beg you to follow me carefully because this is the heart of the case.

You've heard the Prosecutor relate the facts. In essence, now only one thing is certain and undeniable – many men have been killed. We don't know how many exactly because some of them have disappeared. They could have left the country illegally or they could have been killed, buried in a cave in the mountains or eaten by wild animals in the countryside. In fact, a few months ago people found a man's bones on Mount Busambra. His feet were bound with a chain and there was a bullet hole in his skull. The Police could not even establish the man's age with certainty – he could have been thirty or then again fifty years old, he could have been Morabito, the union organizer who disappeared three years ago, or any one of the ex-convicts who disappeared two years ago without leaving any trace...

(He walks out from behind the bench and slowly moves forward.)

Fifty or sixty men killed? Who can say that? This is the only thing that's certain and undeniable: we know nothing else–we don't know what connection exists between one murder and the other; what the exact motive was, nor what links existed between one murder and the other... Some murders occurred in one location, others tens of miles away, in different towns having nothing in common, neither political struggles nor business interests. These towns are not even connected by highway or railroad. Fifty men killed, that's all, fifty bloody bodies of strangers unknown to each other stretched out before us. I will tell you more. The Prosecution did not have the courage to bring those fifty crimes here all together. If he had, he could have exploited the tragic apparatus to its fullest theatricality. No...he patiently selected a few murders, with levity, with cunning, as though he were picking flowers from a meadow. He chose only those murders he thought he could tie neatly together to make a pretty bloody and absurd bouquet. And so, through a macabre fantastic game, the Prosecution has pieced together a case where dozens of men unknown to each other are locked in a cage. They too come from different cities and villages. Everything is glued with a thin thread of saliva, thousands of words, often nonsensical, absurd confessions quickly withdrawn, accusations among people who don't even know each other's names... Finally, the support for all this, and you will see it for yourselves, rests only on one real document, the confession of a man, Rosario Vacirca, the only one that has been confirmed before magistrates…I say to you that this man is insane… but I won't ask you to order a psychiatric evaluation of him right away, but at the end of my cross-examination after I have shown, to satisfy your conscience, that he truly is insane.

(*He returns to his bench and sits down again. At the same time, the Prosecutor calls out the name of the first defendant.*)

PROSECUTOR – We call defendant Luciano Verzì to face the Jury!

(*The second defendant from the left on the top row rises and comes forward. He is a man of average height, dressed in a suit of provincial tastes, well-groomed, short hair, and a neat appearance. He seems very respectful and attentive.*)

PROSECUTOR – Gentlemen of the Jury, many fierce men will come before you, men of incredible moral cruelty, others who were used as instruments of crimes almost blindly, like animals, and others still who made decisions about the lives of human beings as if they were inanimate things. The most brutal was Luciano Verzì. It's right we begin with him because he was the one who committed the first murder, of the union organizer Alicata. But in this story of unchained violence, we find this man always in the middle of it, from the first to the last murder. (*With his hand he slowly moves the dossier before him on the lectern as though reading from it.*)

Luciano Verzì, known as "Pigeon", 36 years old, convicted of crimes against property, attempted murder and acts of violence… Is that you?

VERZÌ – Yes, Sir.

PROSECUTOR – Do you know the charges against you?

VERZÌ – No, Sir. There are many names I don't remember any more, they were people I never met…

PROSECUTOR – Pay attention then. You're accused of premeditated murder of the union organizer Venero Alicata, of simple homicide of the minor Mario Scibilia, of being an accomplice in the aggravated homicides of Giovanni Savoca and Gaetano Nascimbene, of premeditated murder of Chief Inspector Ettore Florena and of being an accomplice in the massacre of eight policemen and soldiers. What say you?

VERZÌ – They're all false accusations. I repeat, I did not even know these men. What motive would I have to kill them?

PROSECUTOR – Since you are innocent, why did you go into hiding?

VERZÌ – My wife told me that four men in plain clothes came looking for me at my house. One said 'Is Luciano Verzì, alias "Pigeon" at home?' 'He is not here', my wife answered. 'When he comes home tell him not to go anywhere because we have to talk to him.' All four made believe they were leaving, but instead two of them hid under the staircase and the other two in the street. But my wife managed to let me know what was happening and so I fled. How did I know who they were and what they wanted from me…?

PROSECUTOR – Had you done something against someone, quarreled with or offended anyone?

VERZÌ – No, your Excellency, no one.

PROSECUTOR – So then, what were you afraid of?

VERZÌ – My head told me to run.

PROSECUTOR – Fifteen days later you were arrested on a train going to the mainland. During the interrogation you confessed to all the crimes of which you stand accused, one by one.

VERZÌ – What could I do, your Excellency? They roughed me up pretty bad.

PROSECUTOR – What do you mean?

VERZÌ – With your permission, Mr. Prosecutor, they slapped my face silly. One grabbed me by the hair while the other questioned me. 'Luciano Verzì, who murdered Venero Alicata?'… When I answered 'How am I supposed to know that?' They let me have the first punch in the face… Then they put my feet inside a box that twisted my toes. There was a handle that twisted my toes when they turned it. One said, 'Luciano Verzi, not only did you murder Venero Alicata, but you also know for sure who killed Francesco Farina and Pietro Garofalo…' and they continued to twist my toes, they punched me on the head and on the mouth, time and time again. I still have the scars. 'Go on, scream!' they kept saying. 'Scream all you want but there's no one who can hear you for a mile…'

PROSECUTOR – Go on!

VERZÌ – You don't believe me, Mr. Prosecutor?

PROSECUTOR – Go on!

VERZÌ – At the end, they left me dying of hunger and thirst. I couldn't even swallow because my mouth was busted up, I couldn't even sit down because as soon as I did they'd start kicking and punching me. Meanwhile they ate, drank, and smoked–'Come, Luciano Verzì, why don't you join us and share this plate of meat and potatoes…? But first you must tell us if it's true that you killed Venero Alicata. Then we'll give you this plate of meat and even a pack of cigarettes.' Mr. Prosecutor, I was foaming at the mouth… What was I supposed to do?

PROSECUTOR – So you confessed that you killed Venero Alicata!

VERZÌ – Yes, Sir.

PROSECUTOR – And you also confessed that you killed Giovanni Savoca and Gaetano Nascimbene!

VERZÌ – It was the same thing! I didn't even know Giovanni Nascinbene. I didn't even know who he was. I still have the scars near my nose and on my head. And medical certificates to prove it…

PROSECUTOR – Then before the pretrial judge you denied everything you had confessed. Nevertheless, you also confirmed to the judge that you knew who had killed Francesco Farina and Pietro Garofalo! Did the judge have you beaten?

VERZÌ – No, Sir! Never!

PROSECUTOR – So you really knew who had killed Francesco Farina and Pietro Garofalo!

VERZÌ – Of course, I knew it, but before I was afraid of saying so to the *carabinieri*. The truth was that I knew it, but I wasn't sure…

PROSECUTOR – And why weren't you sure?

VERZÌ – Because…well… it's not that I had seen them with my own eyes. I knew it because Rosario Mangiagli and Salvatore Salemi had confided in me. They said – 'Do you know who killed Farina and Garofalo? It was Filippo Giacalone!'

(*Suddenly from the defendants' cage one of the accused screams out.*)

DEFENDANT – It's not true!

(*The defendants in the cage start mumbling, but the Prosecutor raps the table lightly with his knuckles twice to restore silence.*)

PROSECUTOR – And then?

VERZÌ – Then nothing! That's it! That's what they said. I didn't believe them and they went away….

PROSECUTOR – We inform the honorable jury that it's no longer possible to verify this episode. Even the defendant knows this…

VERZÌ – That's a good one! What do I know about it?

PROSECUTOR – Rosario Mangiagli and Salvatore Salemi are, in fact, dead. The first was killed as he was getting out of his car and the other was found dead in front of his house…Luciano Verzì, did you know they were dead?

VERZÌ – Yes, Sir! I learned of it afterwards in jail! But they were not friends of mine… I didn't know them well…

PROSECUTOR – But you knew Giovanni Savoca, didn't you?

VERZÌ – Yes, Sir! We were friends, sort of, and when I found out he had been killed, I felt bad. We always played cards together, but he was a tough guy: a bully…

PROSECUTOR – Is that why they killed him, then?

VERZÌ – It could be! What do I know?

PROSECUTOR – You are accused of his murder!

VERZÌ – It's a lie!

PROSECUTOR – You confessed it!

VERZÌ – I told you! They made me confess all kinds of crazy things…

PROSECUTOR – And you are also accused of the murder of Salvatore Nascimbene!

VERZÌ – That's the funniest accusation of all. I did not even know who he was!

PROSECUTOR – He lived a hundred yards from your house!

VERZÌ – Never saw him, never heard his name mentioned.

PROSECUTOR – And you also confessed you killed Chief Inspector Ettore Florena with five shots.

VERZÌ – Yes, Sir, it's true! When you're forced to confess through torture what's the difference if you confess five, six, or seven murders? They told me to confess x number of murders and that's how many I confessed. When they stopped beating me, I stopped confessing. Your Honor, you don't know that it means to stay four nights and four days without food or drink, with broken bones, without a cigarette, forced to stand against a wall, without even a chair…and with me sick and all.

(*He pauses to catch his breath.*)

The truth is that for all the homicides of which I am accused there is not a shred of evidence against me, a single sure proof… nothing! For example, this Police Inspector, what's his name? I did not even know that he existed nor that he had been killed subsequently. I told the pretrial judge that I had an alibi. The night they killed him I had gone with three friends to a funeral of a relative to a town forty kms away.

PROSECUTOR – One of your relatives?

VERZÌ – No, Sir. Of a friend of mine. We left, four of us in one car, at six in the evening. It says so in the transcripts. I can name them…

PROSECUTOR – The Jury ought to know who the other three people were. One is dead and the other two are both accused of murder in this trial… Who else was at the funeral besides these three friends? Anyone who knew you?

VERZÌ – The relatives of the dead man, a bunch of people crying and moaning. But I didn't know anyone because I was not from that town…What did you expect me to do at the funeral? Stop to ask people's names? Dressed in black they all look alike!

PROSECUTOR – Defendant Verzì, you mentioned the transcripts. Did you read the transcripts of your interrogations?

VERZÌ – Yes, Sir. And they are false! I mean that what comes out of them is not true. It's what they forced me to say…

PROSECUTOR – I asked you if you read the transcripts, if you read them with your own eyes?

VERZÌ – No, Sir.

PROSECUTOR – Because you did not want to read them?

VERZÌ – (*With a faint gesture of scorn.*) Because I don't know how to read.

PROSECUTOR – You don't know how to read or write?

VERZÌ – Neither read nor write!

PROSECUTOR – How is that possible? You have a Middle School diploma. Here is your diploma attached to your dossier… Middle School Diploma…

VERZÌ – I needed it when I started working as an assistant in the Medical Insurance office. They told me I had to have a Middle School diploma. So I went out and got myself one…

PROSECUTOR – That is to say, you took the exams and passed them, in spite of the fact that you are illiterate!

VERZÌ – Yes, Sir! There were fifteen other illiterates like me at that examination and they all passed!

PROSECUTOR – And how did that happen?

(*The defendant does not answer. The Prosecutor raises his voice a little.*)

I asked you, how did it happen?

VERZÌ – Mr. Crupi, the lawyer, put in a good word for me with the professors.

PROSECUTOR – Do you know attorney Crupi? Can you point him out, if he is in this courtroom?

VERZÌ – Yes, Sir. He is in the courtroom.

(*The Prosecutor makes a light gesture of dismissal toward the defendant who in turn nods imperceptibly to the Jury and returns to his seat. The Prosecutor meanwhile has begun addressing the Jury.*)

PROSECUTOR – Attorney Emanuele Crupi. We have come to one of the key figures of this trial. The Defense before, faced with the terrifying list of murders, spoke of a bloody and confused mess in which no crime had any logical connection with any other. Before proceeding with the interrogations, I want to show you the frightful concatenation that exists among all the murders. To do so, I must speak to you about two key figures – the first is attorney Emanuele Crupi. Defendant Crupi, I ask you to stand so the Jury can identify you!

(From the lower bench, the third defendant from the left rises and remains standing. He is an elderly man, tall, dressed in black, with gray hair.)

Emanuele Crupi, 68 years of age, attorney, President of the Farmers Union, owner of vast agricultural concerns, accused once thirty years ago of being part of a criminal association, but acquitted in full. This is what we know of him–Emanuele Crupi dominated a large part of the province, in elections he controlled an impressive number of voters, he controlled the nominations and the administrative affairs of almost every public agency, he also surely controlled the market of the areas set aside for urban expansion…

(He nods lightly to the defendant who returns to his seat.)

There is a fact not mentioned in the pages of this trial, which nevertheless is important for you to know. Three years ago, Doctor Giuseppe Salemi the mayor of the city, was killed. There was a trial, but all forty defendants were acquitted. No one ever found out the murderers' names, but that was the sign that a fierce struggle had begun… Some years before the project for the building of a dam in the center of the valley had been presented to the government. It was a monumental work, which would have made it possible to irrigate thirty thousand hectares of land. It would have buried under water, however, most of the citrus groves at the bottom of the valley, including three hundred hectares belonging to defendant Crupi…Mayor Salemi had been the most ardent supporter of the dam and he was killed! Another man even more passionate than Salemi continued to fight to complete that public project–union organizer Venero Alicata. He did not fight only for the dam, but he organized strikes and occupations of land, gave speeches in every part of the province, denouncing building speculations and administrative corruption. I have now come to the second key figure in this trial–Amedeo Barresi! Defendant Barresi, please stand!

(From the top bench the fourth defendant from the left rises. He is a tall man, dressed in gray, with black glasses. He remains motionless.)

Amedeo Barresi, forty five years of age, married, attended only elementary school, former worker in the naval shipyard, formerly employed in the Municipal Assistance Agency, business broker, building contractor, owner of hotels and supermarkets, convicted eight times for violence and false testimony. He was tried for homicide and kidnapping, but he was acquitted. This is what we know of him–in the last ten years he has gained control of nearly all the building zones in the eastern suburbs of Palermo; he has built two hotels, and bought a few retail businesses. He controls the markets of appliances and cement. He probably also controls prostitution and cigarette smuggling in the territory of the province. Union organizer Venero Alicata repeatedly denounced him publicly for corruption and speculation, three times bringing charges against him in court. He also instigated a congressional investigation against him which, however, was never brought to completion…

(*He nods briefly to the defendant who slowly takes his seat again.*)

On the night of October 18, Venero Alicata was shot to death in a deserted street and in the same incident the boy Mario Scibilia lost his life when a bullet hit him on the forehead. We do not know yet if Venero Alicata was killed by order of Emanuele Crupi or by the men of Amedeo Barresi. One fact is certain, though–the ferocious string of murders began when Emanuele Crupi's power ran head on against the equally vicious power of Amedeo Barresi. Venero Alicata who fought both was only the first victim. The massacre continued in a lucid and horrible way. In fact, three individuals operated in the province–Francesco Farina, Pietro Garofalo and Gaetano Nascimbene who speculated in the building industry and perhaps also in the contraband sector. We don't know if they worked alone or together. They were, however, three small-time, daring, and fearless men who seized areas zoned for building, trafficked in cement and became ever more enterprising and daring. Amedeo Barresi had them killed one after the other in the space of fifteen days. Salvatore Nascimbene, however, one of the three men murdered, was a trusted underling of attorney Emanuele Crupi and his murder represented a challenge–it meant that Amedeo Barresi had infiltrated in a bloody way a sector that Emanuele Crupi had controlled without challenge until then. Thus…to reestablish the balance they decided to order the assassination of Carmelo Licitra, a man who worked as a broker for Amedeo Barresi. They chose Giovanni Savoca, an old and absolutely loyal associate, to carry out the revenge. He could not commit the crime personally, however, because he was too well-known, having already two murder convictions on his record. The motive would have been too obvious… so he commissioned the crime to Rosario Vacirca, an unemployed young man… Defendant Vacirca, stand up!

(*From the lower bench the last defendant on the right stands and remains standing without moving. He is nearly in the dark.*)

Giovanni Savoca advanced him five hundred thousand lire in cash, instructed him and sat at the cafe playing cards so everyone could see him there on the night of the murder... Thus Carmelo Licitra fell with his head split open by a shotgun blast fired from three feet away...It's not known who shot him, but who had him killed is clear and barely fifteen days after, the body of Giovanni Savoca, still riding his bicycle, rolled down to the end of a dark street...

(The Prosecutor nods briefly to defendant Rosario Vacirca who returns to his seat.)

In this frightening sequel of murders only one man could have identified the culprits, a man who had collected evidence, bits and pieces provided by informants. That man was Chief Inspector Ettore Florena. No one ever learned why he never used all that evidence and no one knows now whether he had decided finally to use it...but before he could do so, he was killed with six gun shots. There was no limit to the violence then–a building belonging to Emanuele Crupi blew up. Three floors collapsed blinding an old maid who was inside. Then on a trail to Palermo that gloomy Giulietta found with flat tires... they did not manage to deliver it to its destination, but death lay hidden in that trunk, waiting only for someone to come to the appointment...those eight *Carabinieri* and soldiers arrived and the massacre was done.

DEFENSE – *(In a loud voice toward the Jury.)* At that point, Justice went wild! Pressed against the wall by the fear of public opinion, justice which until then had been unable to identify and convict a single person responsible for a hundred murders...suddenly, breathlessly, ran wild...and made a list of crimes that could somehow be tied to the others, bunching together thirty-five human beings inside a cage...

PROSECUTOR – *(Interrupting him brusquely.)* We have all the evidence! The defense knows it.

DEFENSE – We want to hear it now, finally, Mr. Prosecutor.

PROSECUTOR – One at a time! *(He calls out loudly.)* Witness Adriana Miceli!

(The witness enters quickly from the left. She is a young woman dressed with a light leather overcoat. She is frail, pale with delicate though somewhat worn features; faint eye makeup, long hair. She pauses for an instant because she does not know where to go, she shakes a bit, then comes before the Jury.)

PROSECUTOR – Your first and last name and profession?

ADRIANA – Adriana Miceli.

PROSECUTOR – Please, excuse me, but I must ask you to tell us your profession. It's important!

(*The woman hesitates a little. She smiles awkwardly.*)

ADRIANA – Yes, Sir. I…spend time with men! For… money!

DEFENSE – Mr. Prosecutor, the honorable members of the Jury are thinking at this moment – 'Is she a whore, then?' Yes, gentlemen, she is a whore!

PROSECUTOR – I am sorry, but this is important to understand clearly what you are about to say. At any rate, as the honorable defense attorney teaches us, no one here has the right to be scandalized. You are from Rome, aren't you?

ADRIANA – Yes, Sir.

PROSECUTOR – But you live in Palermo…How did you happen to come here?

ADRIANA – (*She shrugs her shoulders lightly.*) I came here seven years ago. At first I lived in a hotel, then I decided to stay and I bought an apartment. Cities are almost all the same. Also, there's the government in Palermo… more activity…

PROSECUTOR – In seven years you certainly met many men. You also named quite a few in your previous depositions…

ADRIANA – They had told me…

PROSECUTOR – Don't worry! I don't want to read these names. I just want... (*Turning to the cage.*) Would defendant Amedeo Barresi please stand? I just want to ask you if you know this man.

ADRIANA – Yes, Sir. I know him.

PROSECUTOR – Were you… I mean, did you have occasion to have intimate relations with him?

(*The witness glances furtively at the cage. She lowers her voice a bit.*)

ADRIANA – Yes, Sir. A few times.

PROSECUTOR – And you have never had any other relations with him, I mean, of a business nature?

ADRIANA – No, Sir. I saw him only a few times. He'd spend part of the afternoon with me, then leave.

PROSECUTOR – What kind of a man did you think he was?

ADRIANA – (*With a little raucous laughter.*) I'd say a woman would have ample reason to be satisfied.

(*Laughter in the cage. Loud and cheerful mumbling.*)

PROSECUTOR – I see your point… However, I was not asking your opinion of his manhood…

ADRIANA – That's what I was talking about….

PROSECUTOR – (*Brusquely.*) Quiet! Wait until you understand the question exactly!

DEFENSE – The Prosecutor is asking you what you thought of him in society.

PROSECUTOR – There! The Defense attorney with his usual clarity has explained the question precisely. So then, what was your opinion of Barresi, what did you think he was?

ADRIANA – A businessman, I think...How could I know? A contractor, in fact, he bought and sold houses...

PROSECUTOR – And how did you judge him?

ADRIANA – (*Hesitantly.*) May I answer? As far as I'm concerned, he was a gentleman!

PROSECUTOR – What is a gentleman for you?

ADRIANA – He paid me well, did not carry on, he was clean, not vulgar or overbearing. Naturally, Your Honor, as you said, I judge men from my perspective. I mean that there are intelligent men who when they go with a woman of pleasure are very amiable and courteous at first, but afterwards they show disgust...Not him...he always continued to be kind, that's why I said he was a gentleman... At any rate, how else could I have known him?

PROSECUTOR – Did you know any of Mr. Barresi's friends?

ADRIANA – I don't think so... I never knew what kind of friends he had...

PROSECUTOR – Somebody must have introduced him to you the first time. Do you remember who he was?

ADRIANA – Yes, Sir. Giovanni Arena. We were in a café in Palermo. At a certain point, Amedeo Barresi walked in, he approached, and began talking with us....

PROSECUTOR – Will you tell us who Giovanni Arena was?

ADRIANA – A friend of mine!

PROSECUTOR – A friend of yours! What kind of friend was he, be more explicit!

ADRIANA – Giovanni Arena was my lover, we lived in the same house.

PROSECUTOR – Were you in love with him?

ADRIANA – (*With sudden harshness.*) Yes, Sir. I was very much in love with him.

PROSECUTOR – (*Also with sudden harshness.*) And did you give him money? How much did you give him, what percentage? Try to be precise down to the penny!

ADRIANA – I gave him half of what I earned from the other men.

He would accompany me with his car, introduce me to clients, protect me…and then as I already said, I was very much in love with him!

PROSECUTOR – Did you give money to other people, too?

ADRIANA – No, Sir, to no one else. Giovanni Arena was the only man I loved…

PROSECUTOR – But you did not know if he was a friend of Amedeo Barresi! He just introduced him to you and that's all!

ADRIANA – I never asked him about the men he introduced to me or where he had met them…

PROSECUTOR – Would you please tell the Jury how and when Giovanni Arena died?

ADRIANA – He was killed a year ago in a street of Palermo with two shotgun blasts from a moving car.

PROSECUTOR – And do you know why he was killed?

ADRIANA – No, Sir. I only know he is dead.

PROSECUTOR – Listen to me carefully! After Arena's death, was there an occasion when Barresi introduced you to a friend of his?

ADRIANA – (*She hesitates.*) Yes, a few times.

PROSECUTOR – And was it Barresi who introduced Luciano Verzì to you?

ADRIANA – (*She hesitates again.*) I don't recall who Verzì is.

PROSECUTOR – Please, approach the cage and look at the people.

ADRIANA – You want me to go near the cage?

PROSECUTOR – Exactly! Go near the cage, yes like that! Now look at the faces of the people in there, look carefully and tell us if you recognize anyone…

ADRIANA – I see Mr. Barresi…

PROSECUTOR – Fine, that is Mr. Barresi… and don't you recognize anyone else? Do you want to look more carefully at the defendants?

ADRIANA – No, I don't know any of them. I can't quite tell…

PROSECUTOR – Let defendant Verzì come out!

(*Verzì comes out and remains two yards away from the woman, looking straight into her eyes.*)

ADRIANA – I don't think so, I don't recall…I've known so many men…

PROSECUTOR – But he admitted knowing you. He stated he came at least four or five times to make love with you…

ADRIANA – Love with me?…Maybe…It's possible... Maybe if I met him in bed I'd recognize him…

(*Laughter in the cage. Even the Defense attorney laughs.*)

ADRIANA – (*Frightened by the laughter.*) I see so many…I mean…

PROSECUTOR – Of course, you can't recognize all the men you meet. But at police headquarters you recognized this man's photo out of three hundred. You singled him out without hesitation–'It's him!'

(*She looks at him frightened.*)

ADRIANA – It could be…but so much time has passed.

PROSECUTOR – Do you recognize him now, yes or no?

ADRIANA – Yes, I recognize him.

PROSECUTOR – And do you recall what you told the police about him?

(*The woman remains silent. She has stopped looking at Luciano Verzì. She does not move.*)

ADRIANA – This is your signed deposition–'Luciano Verzì told me that he had killed union organizer Venero Alicata.' Will you now please repeat that statement, that is, will you confirm or recant your statement? Be very careful about what you say…

ADRIANA – I think he was joking …

PROSECUTOR – A minute ago you hardly recognized his face and now you recall even that he was joking? What do you mean that he was joking?

ADRIANA – The way he told the story it seemed to me that he wanted to joke. I mean that he was lying, clowning…

PROSECUTOR – Tell us the whole story from the beginning…

ADRIANA – We had been together for an hour…

PROSECUTOR – How many days after the murder of Venero Alicata?

ADRIANA – I don't know now…how can I remember that? I think a week or two…The papers still wrote about it…One day he showed up and we spent an hour together…At the end he drank his coffee and stayed in bed smoking. He told me–'Did you read the news about the union man, that elementary school teacher?' 'Who?' I asked, 'the one who got killed?' He continued smoking and looked at me mockingly. 'Do you know who killed him?' he said. 'I killed him!' I started laughing because I thought he was clowning. That's all. The story ended there…

PROSECUTOR – With a laughter?

ADRIANA – Yes, Sir. It was surely a joke.

PROSECUTOR – Why didn't you say that it was surely a joke in the transcripts?

ADRIANA – Your Honor, I was terrified. Even now I am very confused. What have I to do with all of this? I don't even know why I told that story to the police. The Police had persecuted me for a month until I recognized the photo of that man out of hundreds of pictures they kept showing me. Since they learned that I had met that man they started badgering me. Wherever I went cops came. They let clients come in and broke into the room to find them in a compromising position. Each time they kept me locked up a whole day in a hospital room…

PROSECUTOR – Has anyone threatened you recently?

ADRIANA – No, Sir. No one.

PROSECUTOR – Nevertheless, do you confirm now, under oath, that Luciano Verzì told you: – 'I was the one who killed the inspector.'

ADRIANA – (*Softly.*) Yes, Sir.

PROSECUTOR – (*In a loud voice.*) You may go.

(*He nods to the defendant who goes back into the cage, while the prostitute bows hesitantly to the Jury and starts to leave.*)

DEFENSE – (*Suddenly.*) But in your opinion he was joking…

ADRIANA – (*Stopping fearfully.*) Yes, Sir. In my opinion, he was joking…

(*She hesitates, not knowing what exit to take. When the defense points the way out, she hurries toward the left. She disappears while the Prosecutor calls out in a loud voice.*)

PROSECUTOR – Witness Antonino Golino!

(*The witness comes in quickly from the left. He is a man of median height, properly dressed, with tired features, but alert and secure in his demeanor. He stands at attention before the Jury.*)

PROSECUTOR – Antonino Golino, 46 years of age, Sergeant in the Police Judicial unit…

GOLINO – Yes. Sir!

PROSECUTOR – Sergeant, in the last three years you have taken part in almost all police operations. You can provide, therefore, clear picture of the events and the characters involved…

GOLINO – Yes. Sir!

PROSECUTOR – I remind you of the importance of your testimony…

GOLINO – There is no doubt about that!

PROSECUTOR – Well, first of all, I'd like you to answer one question –you know all the serious and horrible events that have occurred–do you believe we are facing random episodes of delinquency or awesome and carefully planned criminal activities? You must have come to a clear conclusion.

GOLINO – Yes, Sir. I have my own idea. Each murder has behind it a hundred other crimes; each murder is a direct consequence of another.

PROSECUTOR – Another question now–citizens almost always believe these bloody phenomena involve only the protagonists themselves, that is, that they only kill one another and that's all! Let me ask you–do these uninterrupted massacres influence the life of society?

DEFENSE – That's a question more appropriately asked of a sociologist!

PROSECUTOR – I want to hear a police sergeant's opinion. Allow me, please... The question is: "What's the meaning of this massacre?"

GOLINO – Mr. Prosecutor, it's a struggle for power!

PROSECUTOR – Power in what sense?

GOLINO – The power to gain control of everything within the territory of a town or even a province...

PROSECUTOR – Be more specific...How does it happen?

GOLINO – In the territory where this occurs not a single thing can happen without their consent...people delude themselves thinking they are free to live as they please, but it's the others who hold them in the palm of their hands and lead them where they will...I don't know if it's clear...They control, for example, the votes in elections, I mean that by shifting two or three thousand votes they can elect a candidate instead of another...they set the price of fruit and fish, they decide if a new store will open in a given street, who will obtain business licenses and building permits...

DEFENSE – Are you really convinced things happen as you say?

GOLINO – Of course, I'm convinced. There can't be any doubts about it. For example, three years ago a contractor decided to buy a lot for a building in a certain area...They explained to him that it was not in his interest to build there, but he insisted on buying the lot and began to build a large structure...One day they grabbed him and they stuffed him inside...

(*He makes a gesture with his hands.*)

How do you call it? One of the conduits used for pouring cement ... but they said nothing for two weeks. They just stuffed him in the conduit and left him there...

DEFENSE – Dead?

PROSECUTOR – Of course, dead! They stuck the body in there without a word. The police searched for the missing man, but meanwhile the structure of the building kept growing; finally, rumors started circulating that the contractor's body was inside one of the cement pylons, but nobody knew which one. They would have had to demolish the entire building and break apart each pylon one at the time. So the building was never finished and no one bought the lot from the heirs…Who would live in a building with a dead man buried somewhere behind one of its walls?

PROSECUTOR – So they control votes in elections, the price of goods and the building zones…

GOLINO – They control everything, even who gets on the list of poor people, the flower business, including the sale of coffins…It's called the *Requiem Eternam* Mafia… There was a man—if I can cite another example—who manufactured biers…and one day he decided to lower his prices, do you follow me?… Everyone considered him a master, a real sculptor. His name was Girolamo Pennisi. He built coffins of great artistic value, all in precious walnut and priced them thirty percent less than the others… how could that be? They shot him on the doorstep of his shop. People started running in terror and for five minutes the street was deserted. This way they even had the time to arrange the body in the coffin, you know … They found him laid out with his arms crossed. They even had time to comb his hair…

PROSECUTOR – Does this kind of power control only political and economic activities or criminal activities as well?

GOLINO – Yes, Sir! Criminal activities, too! Black market and prostitution, for example. It works like this: even whores are favored, sorry, how can I say it? Prostitutes are given preference in all they need. They get housing for them, maids, furniture and clients too and they move them from one section of town to another. They alert them about police raids or intrusions by the vice squad, and finally they protect them from abuses…In exchange they take sixty percent, not a large take when you think that those who ran the houses of prostitution took up to seventy percent… That was very tough going, if you know what I mean…

DEFENSE – Sergeant, did you know that the State collected half of that seventy percent in taxes? Have you an opinion about that, too?

GOLINO – No, Sir! I'm only telling facts, that's all.

PROSECUTOR – And does this Mafia have a name, too?

GOLINO – Yes, Sir! It's called the "Warm bed Mafia." It may seem absurd, but they control almost all the city prostitutes…

PROSECUTOR – Control in what sense?

GOLINO – In the sense that a woman can't be a prostitute in their territory if she has no protection…

DEFENSE – Sergeant, wait a moment, let me understand. So you claim that a beautiful woman, let's say a married woman who lives in that part of town who has marriage problems, needs money or simply gets up one morning and decides 'starting today I want to be a whore'...such a woman can't do it?

(*Mumbling in the cage.*)

GOLINO – It may seem like a joke...but I don't think so.

DEFENSE – Stopping a beautiful woman from being a prostitute! That's what I call a serious violation of her constitutional rights!

(*Cheerful outbursts from the cage, quickly silenced by the Prosecutor.*)

PROSECUTOR – Sergeant, listen carefully now. Do you recognize defendant Luciano Verzì in the cage?

GOLINO – Yes, Sir. Defendant Barresi, Verzì, Filippo Giacalone...

PROSECUTOR – Were you always present when Luciano Verzì was questioned?

GOLINO – Yes, Sir.

PROSECUTOR – Did he confess right away after he was captured?

GOLINO – No, Sir. He didn't say a word for a week. He acted like an animal, but when confronted with defendant Vacirca he had to confess.

PROSECUTOR – Did he confess for all the crimes?

GOLINO – Yes, Sir. All of them! The murders of Giovanni Savoca and Gaetano Nascimbene, of union organizer Venero Alicata and Inspector Florena. He named his accomplices and described the precise circumstances of the crimes, even some we knew nothing about...

DEFENSE – (*Interrupting him.*) Sergeant, is it true that during questioning prisoners can also be savagely beaten?

(*The sergeant remains silent for a moment. He breathes in with a deep sigh.*)

GOLINO – I understand your question...Sometimes certain prisoners, especially the more wild ones, resist...in short, they experience moments of insanity during questioning...

DEFENSE – Sometimes?

GOLINO – Yes, Sir. Especially those who are backed against a wall, that is, who are really guilty of the crimes. Then they rebel and begin breaking furniture, a few hurl themselves with their heads against the glass windows, trying to injure themselves...I don't know if you get my meaning...this way they can claim later that they were tortured.

DEFENSE – What happens in such cases? Do the policemen try to calm them, to persuade them using a benevolent approach?

GOLINO – A few of the prisoners attack the policemen...Once I received a broken arm…they are hoodlums, men who have committed larceny, homicides…what can policemen do? They should not react?

DEFENSE – So, Sergeant, prisoners can be badly beaten…and at the end of the questioning they can have a broken jaw, a wound to the head?

GOLINO – As a rule, no. But it can happen.

DEFENSE – And did Luciano Verzì rebel?

GOLINO – Yes, Sir. He kept quiet without answering the questions, then he would suddenly lunge against the agents and start kicking…when the agents finally managed to subdue him he had epileptic fits, rolling on the floor with foam at his mouth…

DEFENSE – I have here a medical certificate stating that Luciano Verzì really suffers from progressive epilepsy. When he was rolling on the floor, foaming at the mouth, did it ever occur to you to summon a doctor?

GOLINO – No, Sir. We did not call him.

DEFENSE – What did you do then?

GOLINO – We put him in a straight jacket and tied him to the chair…

DEFENSE – Did this take place before or after he confessed? Answer carefully!

GOLINO – Before.

DEFENSE – Then, at a given moment he confessed… I mean, he decided to confess…spontaneously?

GOLINO – I understand this question too…

DEFENSE – And you had no need to put a straight jacket and tie him to the chair. Is that how it went?

GOLINO – I understand this question too…

DEFENSE – Don't tell us that you understand the question; you must give us a clear answer. That's all! After his confession, did Luciano Verzì have occasion to resist, did you have to place him in a straight jacket? In short, did he have occasion to suffer any beatings, albeit involuntary?

(*The sergeant does not answer.*)

Answer the question!

GOLINO – No, Sir.

(*A moment of silence.*)

PROSECUTOR – Thank you, Sergeant.

(*The sergeant stiffens up, bows imperceptibly and turns to leave. The voice of the Prosecutor, however, stops him.*)

PROSECUTOR – I want to ask you another thing–Were you present when defendant Amedeo Barresi was questioned?

GOLINO – Yes. Sir. Nearly always.

PROSECUTOR – Who never confessed, is that right?

GOLINO – No, Sir. Never! We had overwhelming evidence against him, most of all, the confessions by all the others, but he never confessed…

PROSECUTOR – And did he resist during his questioning? Did he suffer epileptic seizures? Was it necessary to tie him to a chair?

GOLINO – No, Sir. Never.

PROSECUTOR – Thank you.

(The sergeant remains at attention for a moment, then he moves away while the Prosecutor calls out.)

PROSECUTOR – Amedeo Barresi!

(The defendant leaves the cage and starts walking unhurriedly. Tall, dressed in a classic dark, elegant suit, a white handkerchief in his breast pocket, a blue tie, very shiny shoes, white cuffs, a gold ring on his finger, a gold watch on his wrist, perfectly combed and lightly glossy hair, and dark metal frame glasses. He seems perfectly at ease and well mannered. He does not swagger, but he appears sure of himself, he speaks slowly, without ever raising his voice and with a certain precise choice of terms. At all times he shows a discreet sense of dignity. As he moves toward the Jury, the whispering in the cage increases.)

PROSECUTOR – silence!

(A hushed silence falls in the room. The defendant, with a light movement of his shoulders and with a light touch of his hand, adjusts his jacket in front. He also looks attentive.)

PROSECUTOR – Will you tell us your personal data?

BARRESI – Amedeo Barresi, 45 years of age, businessman, married.

PROSECUTOR – Amedeo Barresi, you know the charges against you. Criminal association, corruption, false testimony, smuggling, threats and aggravated assaults, multiple premeditated murder. You are accused of being an accomplice in thirteen murders, aggravated by the heinousness of the crime and the importance of the victims.

BARRESI – I declare I am innocent of all charges against me.

PROSECUTOR – Of all the charges?

BARRESI – Yes, Sir, except the charge of threats and violence against Umberto Cimino since it's an event that actually occurred…something that can happen to everyone…

PROSECUTOR – Will you be more precise?

BARRESI – Yes, Sir. Umberto Cimino was a poor fellow I gave a job to and did favors for from the first day I met him. He owed me three hundred thousand lire I had loaned him, but he had refused to pay me back for two years. He never came around. When I met him in Palermo I slapped him. He was a dishonest man. I should have given him three hundred thousand lire worth of slaps, instead I barely gave him enough for one hundred…

PROSECUTOR – You put an economic value on slaps, too?

BARRESI – Money is everything, Your Honor!

PROSECUTOR – Do you know exactly all the other charges against you?

BARRESI – I read the dossier. I studied it carefully.

PROSECUTOR – You are charged as an accomplice in the murders of union organizer Venero Alicata, Francesco Farina, Giovanni Savoca, and finally in the massacre of eight *carabinieri* and military personnel!

BARRESI – I am perfectly aware of them, Your Honor. If it's useful, I can say that personally I did not know any one of these people. You can read the dossier, I know it by heart. There is not a single witness who claims that I knew any of the men who were killed.

PROSECUTOR – For all the crimes you are charged with, you have been accused by five people who are themselves charged with crimes in this trial, and who confessed that they had committed those murders under your orders!

BARRESI – Yes, Sir. They confessed before the police, but when the pretrial judge questioned them, they retracted everything. Some of them admitted that they had never met me. They invented everything to avoid torture.

PROSECUTOR – Yes, but one of them, Rosario Vacirca, confirmed his confession, and you know it.

BARRESI – Of course, I know. I consider him a poor madman. Now he has to prove what he said.

PROSECUTOR – How is it that with ten warrants for your arrest, you never gave yourself up to show your innocence?

BARRESI – Because justice is slow! Before being acquitted an innocent man languishes in jail for two or three years. All that's needed is a miserable wretch to accuse you of something. I've had bitter experiences.

PROSECUTOR – You were captured on the night of May 17 last year in Turin, near death. The police account states you were coming out of a public building with a friend, a car sped past and someone fired a submachine gun against you, wounding you with twelve bullets in the shoulder, in a leg, and in the head.

BARRESI – Who knows who they were trying to shoot at! They mistook me for somebody else and shot me!

PROSECUTOR – A bullet remained lodged in your skull for a month because the surgeons were afraid you could die during the extraction. Before going to the operating table you had occasion to tell the judge that the assassins were Tullio Guarino and Giacomo Manenti, both of whom are also defendants in this trial, and that they had shot you on orders of Emanuele Crupi…

BARRESI – Your Honor, a man with a lead bullet swimming in his skull does not know what the devil he's saying. There are people who do crazy things even if they just have a headache… At that moment, I did not even remember who I was, nor do I remember now what I said.

PROSECUTOR – In the transcript, however, it states clearly that before entering the operating room you lucidly confessed to a priest and you said to the judge who questioned you briefly the following words. I quote "In full consciousness and serenely reconciled with the Lord, I declare that the assassins were Guarino and Manente and both of them were sent by Emanuele Crupi to kill me."

BARRESI – The bullet was swimming in my brain, making me say crazy things. Why should I reconcile myself with the Lord, if I never offended him? That was simply crazy talk…

PROSECUTOR – Amedeo Barresi, you've never met Emanuele Crupi personally, have you?

BARRESI – No, Sir. I had heard his name a few times. I saw him for the first time at this trial…I don't recall which of the defendants told me – 'See that old man there? He's Emanuele Crupi!' That's all.

(*Emanuele Crupi smiles without moving.*)

PROSECUTOR – According to the prosecution, Emanuele Crupi is the man who had four of your friends killed and tried to have you killed in Turin.

BARRESI – There was no motive for doing that. An illogical thing! He does not look like the type who could do such a thing. That night in Turin, who knows who the target was. They shot me by mistake. It can happen to anyone…

PROSECUTOR – But all these things happened to you! You dealt in building lots and your competitors disappeared, your accomplices were found with a load of drugs, four of your friends were killed, they shot you in Turin. Another funny little thing happened to you!

BARRESI – What thing, Mr. Prosecutor?

PROSECUTOR – During the first operation, the surgeons who were extracting the bullet, discovered two other bullets in your body, that is, two strange bullets that had neither entry nor exit wounds. The bullets, in other words, struck you years before and the wounds had healed. How do you explain them?

BARRESI – Mr. Prosecutor, I was unconscious while they operated on me. It could be a mix up, even though I'm convinced that doctors are honest. When they later told me, I thought they were pulling my leg. I have never found a good explanation for it.

PROSECUTOR – Never?

BARRESI – No, Sir. There's only one possibility. It must have happened when I was a boy. I don't remember any more. I used to steal things in the countryside, you know, children do things like that.... And some peasant probably shot me. I may have thought I had been wounded with a stone. How can I remember now what happened? They told me the bullets came from an old pistol, a poor man's gun...

PROSECUTOR – When you were shot, you were returning from France. That's a statement you have never retracted.

BARRESI – Yes, Sir. I was returning from France. I have traveled a lot, I like to make business deals everywhere; most of all I like to see new faces, different people and countries that I don't know. I have been to America, Canada, Mexico. I've seen Agapulco, Vera Cruz, wonderful places, fantastic sights. Mr. Prosecutor, you have probably seen them on TV and you must agree that they're worth the trouble...

PROSECUTOR – You have a lot of money!

BARRESI – Enough to let me do the things I want. Mr. Prosecutor, I have always worked. I started from nothing. Even if it's a crime, I must admit that I adore money. I want to earn as much as I can because money allows me to do or to have all things...

PROSECUTOR – What things, for example?

BARRESI – Everything! Automobiles, friendship, beautiful women, travel, good health. I declared this and it must be in the transcripts–I have a doctor working only for me–the whim of someone who was once terribly poor. I have a great fear of diseases. I'm terrified by them.

PROSECUTOR – Can you tell us precisely the kind of work you do?

BARRESI – Sure. I trade in everything that can be traded. I've bought building lots and built apartments for sale, I've also built two tourist hotels, run gas stations and supermarkets. I also own three stores. I export citrus fruit abroad...and I have all the required licenses, everything is properly registered.

PROSECUTOR – The Tax Department, however, has charged you with tax evasion for eight hundred thousand million lire.

BARRESI – That may be so, Your Honor, I know, but the matter is still under discussion. But in matter of taxes, without offense to anyone, Mr. Prosecutor, even in this room at least eighty percent of the people are cheating the government!

PROSECUTOR – What kind of business did you have in America?

BARRESI – Citrus fruit, there, too. And import and export, in general.

PROSECUTOR – They arrested you once in New York for drug smuggling!

BARRESI – I admit that. They arrested me at the airport as I was returning from Mexico. They locked me in a room, confiscated everything, undressed me completely, they even x-rayed me, but that same evening they set me free with many apologies.

PROSECUTOR – As regards the smuggling charge against the defendant, I think it's important to draw a picture of the situation. In Italy cocaine costs ten times less than in America. In the last two years a single group of smugglers has managed to ship 361 kilos of cocaine from the coasts of Sicily to America earning more than one and a half million dollars. In America the same load of drugs earned for the traffickers more than thirteen million. These figures are also reported in the transcripts, Mr. Barresi, you should recognize them…

BARRESI – I know them, but they don't concern me. I don't even know what heroin is. In elementary school my teacher taught me that heroin is spelled with an "e" at the end and it always referred to Garibaldi's wife…

(*Laughter in the cage.*)

PROSECUTOR – The good humor of a man accused of thirteen murders is not very cheerful!

BARRESI – Mr. Prosecutor, even the confessions of those who accused me of smuggling have been retracted. They have never found a gram of cocaine on me. That day in America, the Police had to return all my baggage, even the box of matches I had and my gun…

PROSECUTOR – So you carried a gun and you had a regular permit for it?

BARRESI – Of course! Why shouldn't I? I travel with a lot of money on me. I had a gun and a regular permit when the *carabinieri* arrested me.

PROSECUTOR – When they arrested you, the *carabinieri* also found a false ID card with your picture, but with a different name and personal data.

BARRESI – It was an old ID card…a boyhood prank. I explained that! I had falsified that card many years before for a reason. Mr. Prosecutor, I don't know if it's really necessary, there are women in the room...but if it's useful... Do you know that once...to get into a house of prostitution you had to be eighteen? Well, I falsified the ID card when I was seventeen, out of love for prostitutes...Something that happened twenty-five years ago...I kept it as a souvenir...what crime is that?

PROSECUTOR – You are very sure of all your things, even the minuscule ones–the right to carry a false ID card, the right to get a regular permit from the authorities and walk around with a gun in your pocket...

BARRESI – If I had the permit to carry a gun, it was certainly my right!

PROSECUTOR – You had a criminal record. You did not have that right!

BARRESI – I had been rehabilitated by serving the sentences.

PROSECUTOR – (*With growing anger.*) Union organizer Venero Alicata accused you of corrupting police officials, and even the clerks in the Police Records Department...

BARRESI – He was saying stupid things.

PROSECUTOR – He accused you of corrupting, tarnishing and bloodying everything you touched.

BARRESI – I didn't even know that man. I never spoke to him.

(*Suddenly the woman dressed in black who had remained seated and without moving in the back of the courtroom, next to the Carabiniere, rises with a terrifying voice. It's Rosalia Savoca, Venero Alicata's mother.*)

ROSALIA –He's the murderer! He's the murderer!

PROSECUTOR – (*Curtly.*) Take her out of the courtroom!

ROSALIA – Can't you hear from his voice... He is the murderer! What are you waiting for?

(*When she feels the Carabiniere's hand on her arm, she emits a lament like a scream of pain.*)

ROSALIA – What kind of man are you? Can't you see he is spitting in your faces?

(*She buries her head in her shoulders as the Carabiniere leads her away toward the door. Barresi meanwhile has not moved, remaining immobile and looking straight, without turning around.*)

BARRESI – (*His voice slightly changed.*) I've been rehabilitated by serving all sentences...

PROSECUTOR – (*Interrupting him.*) I believe it's useful to recall that defendant Amedeo Barresi, before this trial, in the last twenty years, has been sentenced numberless times for violence, extortion, false testimony, and he has been indicted nine times for homicide, attempted homicide and kidnapping....

DEFENSE—And acquitted as many times in a court of law!

PROSECUTOR – That is true, but it's also true that neither I nor you, Attorney for the defense, nor any member of the Jury, have ever been indicted in our lives nine times for homicide, criminal association and finally for thirteen savage murders...

BARRESI – I have been unlucky, Mr. Prosecutor; in life there are the poor and the rich and there are lucky and unlucky people. I am involved in risky business deals, I have to deal with people with a mean disposition. And many times I have been unlucky....

PROSECUTOR – Let the Jury keep in mind the poor luck of the defendant–he owns sixty apartments, three large retail stores, a building company, five automobiles, a hotel and a villa valued at more than two million dollars...

BARRESI – (*With a slight tinge of anger in his voice.*) And since I own these things, it must mean that I am a delinquent, a murderer, and a ruffian. Mr. Prosecutor, if you are claiming that I succeeded in having two million dollars in my pocket because I am a murderer, a thief, and a ruffian, you must prove it. I can only tell you one thing: they accused me nine times for murder and they acquitted me nine times. Thus, there are two possibilities–either I'm really innocent and I deserve to walk around with a pistol in my pocket, or I am indeed a hoodlum and all nine times the judges who acquitted me were paid off or were afraid!

PROSECUTOR – (*Harshly.*) This could cost you another serious charge of contempt of Court!

BARRESI – (*His voice is quivering a little. He tries to control himself.*) I beg your pardon, Your Honor. But I have been locked up in a cell for eleven months. You can't even imagine what a filthy place jail is, sleeping next to miserable and dirty people. I have been ill twice. I asked the *carabinieri* to bring me a cup of coffee eight hours ago...as a courtesy... or don't I have the right to ask them to bring me a cup of coffee?

PROSECUTOR – (*Cutting him short, harshly and in a loud voice.*) Bring in Mrs. Alicata, the mother of union organizer Venero Alicata.

DEFENSE—The defendant is too tired. This is a confrontation that makes no sense!

BARRESI – (*With a light smile, courteously.*) No, no, Sir. I'm not tired... Everything that needs to be done...

(Deep silence in the courtroom. The woman has appeared next to the defendants' cage and the Prosecutor motions to her to come forward. She remains motionless in her blackness before the Jury, staring directly at the face of Amedeo Barresi. He does not turn around and continues to look straight.)

PROSECUTOR – Rosalia Savoca, widow Alicata, 57 years of age, farmer…

(The woman listens to him unmoving, without taking his eyes off Amedeo Barresi. She answers in a low voice.)

ROSALIA – Yes, Sir.

PROSECUTOR – Your son, Venero Alicata, had taught for a few years in rural schools as an elementary school teacher, then he became a union organizer. Also he was arrested twice for inciting a riot and for the occupation of building sites. He was killed on the night of October 18, with five gun shots… Is this correct?

ROSALIA – Yes, Sir.

PROSECUTOR – Do you know if he ever felt in danger?

ROSALIA – My son was sure they would kill him. But he continued his fight. When he was a boy, my husband and I went hungry to send him to school, first to the seminary and then to Teacher's College. If he had remained a farmer, he would still be alive…

PROSECUTOR – This was your only son?

ROSALIA – Yes, Sir.

PROSECUTOR – Why was he afraid of being killed?

ROSALIA –He had given a speech one evening in a town and that same night, as he was leaving, some men wearing hoods turned his car over and began to beat him. They broke one of his arms…

PROSECUTOR – But did anyone ever threaten him, I mean, anyone whose name he knew? How did he know they were going to kill him…Who was going to kill him?

ROSALIA – Yes, Sir, he knew…

(She does not continue speaking. She seems in a trance looking at Amedeo Barresi.)

PROSECUTOR – Go on, Mrs. Savoca…

(The woman turns around slowly.)

ROSALIA – Six days before he was killed, my son…

DEFENSE – (*Interrupting her.*) Madam, this is already in the transcripts and there is no evidence…

ROSALIA – (*In a very loud voice, a shriek.*) Six days before being killed, my son knew it. He knew it!

(*She leans forward imperceptibly moaning softly as though she were catching her breath.*)

One evening, six days before being killed, my son did not return home…and I waited for him until three in the morning…

DEFENSE – Madam, it's already in the transcripts and there is no evidence…

ROSALIA – (*With the same voice as before, as though she did not hear the interruption.*) He returned at three AM and told me that three men had pointed a gun at him and had made him climb into a car…Luciano Verzì, Carmelo Licitra and Amedeo Barresi were there …

DEFENSE – Have you ever considered your son might have invented these things?

ROSALIA – (*With a voice that keeps getting louder.*) Amedeo Barresi was there and offered him money…

(*She is quiet for a moment as if to concentrate. Her gaze is again fixed on Barresi's face.*)

He told him – 'Idiot, why do you persist in harassing me? I can give you all the money you want…' And while my son related these things that night, he was pale as a ghost… He had been sick for some time, he could not sleep at night…I understood that he was afraid. This was an awful thing for me because I could not help him… You cannot understand, I was an old and illiterate peasant and he was a teacher. Whenever he spoke in public there were at least ten thousand people there. And I could not do a thing for him. This is my sorrow….I was his mother and I let him go to his death. The night when the *carabinieri* told me he had been killed, they didn't want me to see how he was… And how can you stop Rosalia Alicata from seeing her son? He was in the middle of the street with his arms wide open, his face and his chest all covered with blood… Ahhhh!

(*Suddenly she begins to weep, moaning and continuing to stare at Barresi's face.*)

Amedeo Barresi, I would like to see you dead like that!

(*Amedeo Barresi continues to look before him, without turning around.*)

BARRESI – Rosalia Alicata, when your son was killed I was in France. You must accept the facts. I have the evidence… the stamp on my passport.

ROSALIA – Every day I would like to see you dead like that!

(*With desperation in her voice.*)

Every day, like that, before my eyes!

BARRESI – (*reacting against her.*) Rosalia Alicata, I was not there! It was your son who challenged death!

ROSALIA – You were his death!

BARRESI – Mr. Prosecutor, this woman is insane.

ROSALIA – You had him killed! You had him killed!

(*She takes a few steps toward the defendants' cage, looking at their faces. She lets out a heart-rending scream.*)

Who among you has the courage to come forward and say this is not true? I am Venero Alicata's mother and I am not afraid of you.

(*She feels the hand of the Carabiniere on her arm and pulls away from him sharply, with a moan, as though she felt disgust. Following the thrust of that gesture, she exits from the left, leaving the courtroom in deep silence.*)

PROSECUTOR – "It was your son who challenged death!" That's what you told her. What did you mean?

BARRESI – Everybody knew it, everybody said it. He brought charges, gave speeches, incited people, continuously hurling insults…I said simply what I heard others say…what do I know?

(*He takes off his glasses. He is shaking lightly.*)

Now I am really tired, Mr. Prosecutor. I have a fever.

PROSECUTOR – You may go. We will call you back. We call defendant Filippo Giacalone to the stand.

(*Amedeo Barresi bows lightly before the Jury and puts on his glasses again. He returns to his seat and stays there without moving. Meanwhile Filippo Giacalone has come forward – a small man with long hair, a worn face, an old red tie. He came forward excitedly making little superfluous gestures, looking around anxiously with a pale smile. He stares at the Prosecutor in awe.*)

GIACALONE – Filippo Giacalone, 37 years of age…

PROSECUTOR – One moment!

GIACALONE – Yes, Sir.

(*The Prosecutor is leafing through the dossier and Giacalone waits with trepidation. He turns around to look toward the cage with a hesitant smile and tries to maintain his composure as much as possible. He stares at the Prosecutor with deference.*)

PROSECUTOR – This is Filippo Giacalone. Pay close attention. He is one of the typical defendants in this trial, in deed, the epitome of Mafia delinquency, not so much for his real importance as for his instinctive criminal vocation, for the brutish facility with which he, blindly driven, committed the most heinous crimes. Filippo Giacalone, by his own confession, stands accused of driving and abandoning the car loaded with explosives that killed the eight military personnel. He is also accused of participating in three consecutive killings within a week – the murder of Gaetano Nascimbene, in full daylight, in front of his house with a shotgun blast to the back of the head from three yards away; the murder of Francesco Farina and Pietro Garofalo, which took place four days after at dawn on a street at the outskirts of the city where the victims were riding a motorcycle. Brought down with shotgun blasts, the victims were finished off with a pistol point blank…There is an oddity worth noting–the defendant confessed he was alone when he killed Gaetano Nascimbene, but defendant Luciano Verzì also confessed responsibility for the same murder.

DEFENSE – A man killed twice by two different people! A unique case, Mr. Prosecutor–the police managed to obtain astonishing confessions…

PROSECUTOR – We have overwhelming evidence against Giacalone. As regards the massacre of the military personnel we have his detailed confession, offered freely the same night of his arrest, when we had eight other people under arrest and no precise clues had emerged pointing to him. As regards the double homicide, the evidence relies heavily on the other defendants' testimony who stated they saw him fleeing the crime scene, or that they learned from him the circumstances and motives for the double homicide, when he asked for their protection and for money to leave the country… Giacalone stay still!

(*Giacalone has been showing signs of restlessness and anguish, moving his legs, pounding his fist against the palm of his other hand. When the Prosecutor reprimands him, he stiffens up.*)

PROSECUTOR – The Defense asked for a psychiatric evaluation of Filippo Giacalone even before the trial began, but the request was rejected. Listen, however, to the District Attorney's description of Giacalone–"Filippo Giacalone is an individual with low moral and mental aptitudes in whom the lack of education accentuates his psychological shortcomings. A habitual thief, liar, deserter, compulsive liar, vice-ridden, he contracted a serious venereal disease. He has been sentenced eleven times for theft, eight times for purse-snatching and petty thievery. While he has the capacity to understand and make decisions, he manifests a vocation for delinquency of the basest kind. He is now unredeemable. He has confessed his guilt for all the crimes attributed to him in the dossier…"

(*A moment of silence.*)

Are you Filippo Giacalone, 37 years of age, known as "Little Christ," door-to-door salesman, etc…etc…?

GIACALONE – Yes, Sir. I'm Filippo Giacalone.

PROSECUTOR – Why do they call you "Little Christ"?

GIACALONE – That's how they call me.

PROSECUTOR – I mean why "Little Christ"? What does it mean?

GIACALONE – It means probably a fellow who is persecuted, a sort of suffering Christ...What do I know?

(*Whispering and laughter from the cage. Even the defendant hints an anguished laughter. The prosecutor raps his knuckles lightly on the table.*)

GIACALONE – Mr. Prosecutor, they're making me laugh…

PROSECUTOR – Silence! So, Giacalone, you stand accused of multiple aggravated homicides, homicide of Gaetano Nascimbene, and the double homicide of Francesco Farina and Pietro Garofalo. Furthermore you are accused of falsifying personal data, carrying illegal arms, traffic violations, resisting arrest and aggravated theft….

GIACALONE – Mr. Prosecutor, I am completely innocent!

PROSECUTOR – Listen, Giacalone! It's useless to read you the transcripts. You know them already. Not only did you confess, but four of the defendants clearly accuse you of the double homicide. Did the police torture you, too, before you confessed?

GIACALONE – Mr. Prosecutor, I have to tell the truth. As soon as I went into the police headquarters for questioning I got a dislocated jaw from the first punch. There was a policeman named Masuzzo, a cop from Messina, with moustaches who said he was real mean. He asked me my name, profession, etc.. 'Filippo Giacalone, door-to-door salesman,' and right away he punched me in the mouth. After that, I tell you the truth, I confessed right away…

PROSECUTOR – Without being tortured?

GIACALONE – Yes, Sir. After the first punch! What purpose would it have served? All the others had told me–'Confess everything they want. If they say you killed this guy or the other, confess right away. If you don't, they'll break your bones. In any case–don't you know?–these confessions are not worth anything!'

PROSECUTOR – And then?

GIACALONE – Then, nothing, Mr. Prosecutor. They questioned me the whole night. The *carabinieri* even gave two cups of coffee and a pack of cigarettes. "Good, Giacalone!" they kept saying. And now I'm here.

PROSECUTOR – Indicted for eleven aggravated murders!

GIACALONE – (*With a slight hint of desperation.*) 'Good, Giacalone!' yea, right!

(*With a tone of rebellion in his voice.*)

Mr. Prosecutor, all the statements in the transcripts are not true!

PROSECUTOR – (*Reacting harshly.*) What do you mean, they're not true? You were captured with a gun in your hands, in your wallet you had a fake identity card, you started kicking the arresting officers, they found a hundred kilos of American contraband cigarettes in your house, you broke the lock in your cell to escape…

GIACALONE – But I never killed anyone, that's the important thing!

PROSECUTOR – You drove the Giulietta loaded with explosives to the place of the massacre. You confessed that you stole the car without knowing it contained a trunk full of dynamite…Who told you to steal that car?

GIACALONE – I did not steal the car.

PROSECUTOR – Giacalone, you are digging your own grave! The same night of your arrest you gave the license plate of the Giulietta. You had memorized it!

GIACALONE – I had read it in the papers…

PROSECUTOR – The exact license plate had not been made public by any paper. Finally among the ruins of the explosion they found a piece of your scarf. Giacalone, don't you understand we have the proof?

(*The defendant is silent.*)

Maybe you told the truth...you didn't even know there was dynamite in the car… but you must tell us then who ordered you to steal it…

(*The defendant is silent.*)

There is no way out for you, Giacalone. This way you can't even throw yourself at the mercy of the Court. Also we have the evidence for the other murders (*insisting.*)…Do you know Antonino Gagliano?

PROSECUTOR – (*Before he can answer.*) Do you know Giacomo Colosi?

GIACALONE – Yes, Sir.

PROSECUTOR – (*Always with the same tone.*) And what about Luciano Verzì? Come on, Giacalone! If I ask them to come before you, would you recognize them?

GIACALONE – (*Frightened.*) Of course, I would recognize them.

(*He turns around as he hears the three defendants coming out of the cage at the request of the Prosecutor. They line up in silence about three yards away from Giacalone.*)

PROSECUTOR – (*In a loud voice.*) Antonino Gagliano, I am reading from your deposition – "The day when Francesco Farina and Pietro Garofalo were killed, precisely two minutes afterwards, I saw Filippo Giacalone fleeing on a motorcycle. I called out to him but he did not even stop...." Is this true or false?

GAGLIANO – I thought it was him.

PROSECUTOR – Was it him or not?

GAGLIANO – (*Looking at Giacalone in the face.*) Yes, Sir. It was him.

PROSECUTOR – (*In a loud voice.*) Giacomo Colosi, you too declared you saw Giacalone fleeing on a motorcycle from the street where two minutes before the double homicide had been committed.

COLOSI – (*Calmly.*) Yes, Sir. I saw him.

GIACALONE – (*Shaking.*) It's not true, it's not true! I was simply running away like everybody else because I was afraid the police were coming. I had a record...

PROSECUTOR – (*Overpowering him with his voice.*) Giacalone, listen to what this other friend of yours has to say. Luciano Verzì, repeat now what you declared before the judge!

VERZÌ – (*He nods lightly, he fixes his jacket.*) The same night when Pietro Garofalo and Francesco Farina were killed the police rounded up thirty of us, but after a week they released us because they had no evidence at all. Four or five days afterwards Filippo Giacalone came to see me and told me – "I killed Farina and Garofalo."

PROSECUTOR – Is that what he said exactly?

VERZÌ – Yes, Sir. Exactly as I said. To tell you the truth, I was very surprised because I knew Giacalone and considered him inept, incapable of it, your Honor, a good man, innocuous. He told me–"Now I need help, at least five hundred dollars to leave the country..."

GIACALONE – It's not true, Your Honor...It's not true! I was only afraid of being arrested, I had a prior record, I felt the police on my heels and that's why I asked him for the money, a hundred fifty dollars...

(*Turning to Verzì suddenly.*)

You're a dishonest man, a man without honor...you had Farina and Garofalo killed! You all killed them and now you're sending me to jail in your places. Am I capable of killing a man, go on, say it! Was I capable of killing anyone?

(*The three men look at him without saying a word.*)

VERZÌ – Is this the way you show your gratitude, Giacalone? Your wife and children were dying of starvation and I gave them three hundred dollars out of pity. I'm paying for your lawyer and this is the way you say thanks? What kind of a pitiful man are you?

PROSECUTOR – Why are you paying for his lawyer?

VERZÌ – Because I took pity on him. Because he asked me when they arrested him. His wife came crying to my house! Ask him!

GIACALONE – That's a lie! My wife doesn't even know him.

VERZÌ – (*Calmly.*) His wife's name is Carmela Mendolia, she is thirty-two years old and she has been sentenced twice for abandonment of her conjugal home. She has black hair, black eyes. What else do I need to tell you? Carmela Mendolia came to my house to beg me – "You have to lend me three hundred dollars because we have no more money to pay the rent." She kept saying – "My husband got himself arrested…but you must do this act of charity for us." So because I knew the family I loaned her three hundred dollars lire. I took pity on her.

GIACALONE – (*Takes a step forward, in desperation.*) Lies, lies!

VERZÌ – So then ask your wife to tell you who gave her the money…how she is feeding your children…

(*Cheerful whispering in the cage that the Prosecutor quells by rapping his knuckles on the table.*)

PROSECUTOR – Silence!…You can go!

(*He nods to the three defendants and they slowly return to their seats in the cage. Giacalone has an outburst.*)

GIACALONE – Mr. Prosecutor, one of these days they will kill me inside the prison. They threaten me with knives every day…

PROSECUTOR – They have knives in prison? Who has the knives?

GIACALONE – Yes, Sir. During the exercise hour in the courtyard they surround me and they point a knife to my stomach – "If you talk, you're dead!"

PROSECUTOR – Who are they? Tell us!

GIACALONE – (*The defendant remains silent, then lets out a soft moan.*) Mr. Prosecutor, I am ill, every night I get a 102 fever and they refuse to take me to the infirmary. Even the guards are persecuting me…I even wrote a complaint to the Warden…

(*The Prosecutor curtly interrupts him.*)

PROSECUTOR – In the course of your confession you also told the police the motives for the double homicide. Do you remember them?

(*The defendant is silent. He is frightened and hesitant.*)

You said that Farina and Garofalo were persecuting you. You wanted to register in the Christian Democratic Party, but they threatened to reveal that you'd been a member of the Communist Party…

GIACALONE – That was a joke I made up during the confession. But can you imagine that I would kill two men for something like that?

PROSECUTOR – But the records show that in the last ten years you have been registered in four different political parties.

GIACALONE – Mr. Prosecutor, after the war, everybody did that in my hometown. When the war ended, it was a real messy situation. Everybody believed they could gain power and made threats – the Communists, the Christian Democrats, the Monarchists... The Fascists had disappeared and therefore, everyone tried to grab as much as they could, trying to understand who was the strongest…Your Honor, I don't know where you were then…I mean, Your Honor, I saw men like you changing party overnight – 'Giacalone, you have to vote for the King! Is it possible you have no sense?' And a month later – 'Dummy, you haven't got a cent and you want to vote against the Communists?' I am an illiterate. Even if I wanted to get a permit to sell door to door I had to depend on those who know how to get such things. I tried to understand which party was better for me…at first I was for the Monarchists, then I thought the Communists would win, finally the Christian Democrats showed up…What was I supposed to do? What does this have to do with murder?

PROSECUTOR – You may return to your seat, Giacalone…You have only one chance! You have to reveal who ordered you to steal that car!

GIACALONE – Your Honor, I'm a sick man. Please send me to the infirmary…

PROSECUTOR – Did the prison doctor examine you?

When the prison doctor says so, you will be transferred to the infirmary… Return to your seat.

(*Giacalone hesitates.*)

GIACALONE – Yes, Sir.

(*He hesitates again.*)

Do you know what the truth is, Mr. Prosecutor? That I am nothing. Nobody protects me, I have no gangster friends and I'm not a gangster. I am a thief, I have falsified my papers, but I am zero, I'm a coward, I've never rebelled…You can't understand what the life of a worthless man is like, a man who has no protection and is not capable of rebelling, not even if they kick him in the stomach. He is worthless, like a dog.

(Whispering and laughter in the cage, quickly silenced by the Prosecutor with a light rapping of his knuckles on the table. Giacalone has a faint smile on his lips and nods in acquiescence.)

GIACALONE – Can you see what they're doing to me now? They're capable of killing my children – they already told me…I wish I had the courage, if I get out of here, to wait for them in front of their houses and shoot them in the face, one by one. You know, Mr. Prosecutor, when I heard that one of them had killed an enemy of his, I envied him!…

(He cannot say anything else and understanding that he has to go, he awkwardly clicks his heels to take his leave.)

Yes, Sir.

(He hesitates, he is agitated with anger and fear, he attempts a faint and sorrowful smile.)

Mr. Prosecutor, I'm innocent!
PROSECUTOR – Giacalone, you said what you had to say…You may return to your seat.

(Giacalone stands still without speaking. He repeats with the same tone of voice as before.)

GIACALONE – I'm innocent!

(Again he awkwardly clicks his heels.)

Yes, Sir.

(Starts to move toward the cage, but suddenly he has a brief outburst against Luciano Verzì seated among the other defendants.)

GIACALONE – Luciano Verzì, what kind of a man are you? I was asking you the hundred and fifty dollars as an act of charity. Why do you want to ruin me?

(Feverishly, with short frightened outbursts against the other defendants.)

Antonino Gagliano, you tell them that I'm innocent. Mr. Crupi, Excellency, you've known me since I was a child…am I capable of killing anyone?

(The defendants remain motionless.)

Is it possible you're all against me? Mr. Prosecutor, they all know…call them one by one again, make them confess! Come on, why doesn't anybody want to help me? What did I do to you?

(*He moans imperceptibly, he is exhausted. Suddenly, he turns to the Jury, screaming.*)

I'm innocent, I am innocent!
PROSECUTOR – You must tell us who told you to steal that car!
GIACALONE – You have no pity for me?

(*He falls to his knees.*)

PROSECUTOR – (*In a loud and harsh voice.*) Giacalone, you must tell us who ordered you to steal that car!

(*Giacalone catches a glimpse of the carabiniere next to him and while still on his knees moves backwards to avoid being touched. He gets to his feet with a shudder and returns quickly to his seat and remains there unmoving among the other defendants. They are all motionless and silent in the shadows. And the curtain falls.*)

Act II

(The same Courtroom, on a different day and at a different hour of the day. From unseen windows far above a different, brighter and more profound light comes down as in a church. Some corners of the hall are starkly lit while others remain in shadows. The end wall is bare and remains almost totally dark. On the far end, next to the empty bench there is a carabiniere. On the foreground, before the Court, a chair. The defendants are motionless and silent.

Suddenly a man comes forward from the left. He is dressed in black. He has long and somewhat ruffled hair, and old-fashioned eyeglasses. He moves forward hesitantly, first going in the wrong direction, toward the Prosecutor, then pausing for a moment and moving quickly toward the chair. He sits down facing the Court, adjusts his eyeglasses with the tip of his index finger, and waits without even moving his eyes.)

PROSECUTOR – Only two sessions remain before the debate and the sentencing. They will be reserved to the principal defendants, and therefore to the essential proofs of the trial: this session to defendant Emanuele Crupi and the last one to Rosario Vacirca. Prior to calling defendant Crupi before the Court, we need to hear a witness who will shed light on this defendant's personality: professor Luciano Salemi, Giuseppe Salemi's brother who was the mayor of the city, killed three years ago.

(At the sound of his name, the witness stood up and remained almost at attention, with his shoulders leaning forward.)

PROSECUTOR – Are you professor Luciano Salemi, 36 years old?
SALEMI:–Yes!
PROSECUTOR – You may sit down!
SALEMI – Thank you!

(The witness sits. Even though he does not move, the tone of his voice betrays his nervousness.)

PROSECUTOR – You know many of the defendants in this trial and the events that preceded it! You also know that this long tragedy began with a crime that's not being tried in this chamber, but which nevertheless was the its starting point: the murder of the city's mayor, doctor Giuseppe Salemi, your brother...
SALEMI – In a way.
DEFENSE – What do you mean, "in a way"?
SALEMI – I mean that I don't know if there's any connection between

my brother's murder and the other crimes. I cannot enlighten the Court! I don't know who killed my brother; there was never any proof. I can only relate what happened, if that can be useful to you.

DEFENSE – So you can't make a clear accusation, and provide the proof! In other words, you can't point to a man and say: "He is the murderer!" And you can't even say if there's any connection between that crime and the facts of this trials….

SALEMI – No, Sir, I cannot!

DEFENSE – So then, what is the point... What's the sense of all this...?

PROSECUTOR – Anything that can make us understand how things happened and why, is useful to us... Witness Salemi, tell us the facts as you know them!

(*He nods to the witness.*)

SALEMI – Five years ago my brother was elected mayor. He was a doctor, an obsessed politician, he fought hard for two months giving as many as five speeches a day. He hardly slept. He wasn't much in terms of his education and culture, did not have great administrative skills, but he was a good looking man, tall, passionate, he had the knack for making people like him and had a kind of visceral love for his town. Finally, he was an honest man...

DEFENSE – What does it mean to be an honest man?

SALEMI – I mean that he never took advantage of his position to line his pockets, to favor his family. He had an obsession for justice...The night he was elected, the people organized a big demonstration, a torchlight procession. He held the town in the palm of his hands... Not only was he the mayor, but he was also the district secretary for the political party that had won the election. He seemed to have complete mastery of the town... One year after the election, instead, his political power stood on shaky ground. In reality, that same day he had begun to die... A group of people applied for membership in my brother's party, but he rejected their requests...

PROSECUTOR – Why?

SALEMI – Because they belonged to other parties that until then had held the majority in town. They were men without ideals who had understood that the decline of their party was irrevocable and they needed to be part of the strongest party again... They controlled at least five or six thousand votes, with which the party could have obtained a crushing majority in the whole district. My brother, however, refused to give them membership cards.

DEFENSE – Let me understand! Masses of voters freely switch their allegiance from one party to another. It happens everywhere. People can change their minds out of conviction. If these movements of political influence didn't occur, all elections would produce the same results... Or does the witness believe that a citizen who is disillusioned with a party should continue to suffer harm for the sake of coherence?

(*The witness doesn't answer.*)

DEFENSE – Did they threaten your brother?

SALEMI – No, never! They applied again in greater numbers. The first application contained only eighty signatures; the second had more than five hundred... They turned to the national political secretary and got their membership cards...

PROSECUTOR – Does the witness recognize any of those people among the defendants in this Courtroom?

SALEMI – Yes, Sir! Attorney Emanuele Crupi was the most prominent in the group! He alone controlled at least four thousand votes... Attorney Mario Zaccaria who is now in the Chamber of Deputies, Professor Alimeno who was a Deputy and President of the Province...

DEFENSE – Both of whom are not defendants here, let's make it clear! They are both men of considerable political and social prestige...

SALEMI – I am relating the facts!

DEFENSE – Let's hear them, then!

SALEMI – My brother was elected with sixteen thousand votes. Only a few hundred, however, were people registered in his party. He quickly found himself in the minority within his own political party. As mayor he could do only what the others wanted him to do...

PROSECUTOR – What did the others want?

SALEMI – Everything you can want, everything you can do... Decide what new personnel to hire, choose the commission for competitive bidding, award contracts for road maintenance, choose public works projects, decide whom to hire as janitors and street cleaners, compile the list of indigent people. There's a lot you can do...

DEFENSE – And what ideas did the witness' brother have regarding these things? He had no special projects, no recommendations to make, no contracts, or bids to take care of?

(*The witness remains silent.*)

DEFENSE – He had no licenses to grant, no friends to find jobs for...?

SALEMI – I didn't say the others wanted to do all these things. I said the things you can do when you have a city in your hands. I am relating the facts, that's all!

DEFENSE – Let's hear them!

SALEMI – My brother went to the Party's provincial secretary to appeal the membership granted to that group of people, and then he turned to the national secretary...

DEFENSE – How many people received membership?

SALEMI – I already told you. More than five hundred!

DEFENSE – And how many votes, in real terms, did they represent?

SALEMI – I can't say precisely. At least eight or nine thousand votes in the district, but they had alliances and other votes in the whole province...

DEFENSE – Since you are relating facts, as you say, do you think that a party could refuse eight or nine thousand votes for the mere presumption of political insincerity? Haven't we seen sensational publicity for the banal episode of a citizen ripping up his party's membership card to join another. Are you aware of this?

SALEMI – I am not judging whether my brother acted correctly or wrongly in fighting against those men. I am only relating what happened...

PROSECUTOR – Did you hold a political office during that period?

SALEMI – Yes, I was Councilman in the ruling party, but I did not have my brother's interests nor his passion...

DEFENSE – And even during that period, were death threats made against your brother?

SALEMI – No, never! But he understood that death was in the air; people no longer showed him the same respect. As his isolation grew, so grew his stubborn obsession. They offered him the chance to resign in exchange for a new position in a Palermo agency, but he refused; he knew they were beginning to compile the lists of candidates for Parliament and they wanted him out of the way. He wrote a petition to the national party secretary, he made a list of names and of things that his enemies were trying to obtain...

PROSECUTOR – What things?

SALEMI – All the things that can be obtained! I already mentioned them...

PROSECUTOR – Please, repeat them, giving specific examples!

SALEMI – For instance, a long panoramic road that would have enhanced the value of almost a thousand hectares of land zoned for building, the failure of the dam project, the hiring of all the personnel in the Health Care Department and in the agricultural cooperatives... He sent that petition to the national party secretary. He always carried a weapon and was accompanied by one of his friends, Sebastiano Crucillà, a political fanatic like him.

They both carried guns in their pockets and sawed-off shotguns hidden under their coats.

PROSECUTOR – When he went out at night, did you accompany him...?

SALEMI – No, in the last days, never! I was afraid, I did not have his passion...

DEFENSE – Passion for what?

(*The witness does not reply.*)

DEFENSE – Is this why your brother despised you?

(*The witness does not reply.*)

PROSECUTOR – Continue!

SALEMI – One night he went to the club with his friend. The club was in the square and they were about to cross it. It was exactly 9:18 P.M. Suddenly the whole town was blacked out and soon after that, bursts of submachine gun and rifle shots were heard. The people barred themselves in their houses... After five minutes the lights came back on and my brother was dead in the middle of the square, along with Sebastiano Crucillà. They counted 63 bullet holes on their bodies...

PROSECUTOR – What happened next?

SALEMI – Nothing! My brother was given a solemn funeral attended by the most prominent members of his party. They made a collection to erect a small monument in the cemetery, and they named a side street in town after Giuseppe Salemi...

DEFENSE – Was anyone indicted for the two murders?

SALEMI – Eighteen people were indicted, but they were acquitted for not committing the crime!

PROSECUTOR – Professor Salemi, in the preliminary questioning you stated once that your brother had written a detailed account addressed to the Justice Department and to the *carabinieri* to denounce the abuses of power and corruption that had taken place. He also named those who had a motive for killing him...and provided the proof...

SALEMI – I cannot confirm this with certainty...

(*The prosecutor harshly interrupts him.*)

PROSECUTOR – You stated this before the judge!

(*The witness hesitates. He slowly removes his eyeglasses.*)

SALEMI – I meant to say... I knew that my brother intended to write a detailed account, a diary. He had been saying it for a long time...every now and then he'd show me a file...

PROSECUTOR – And what was written in it?

SALEMI – (*Hurriedly*) – I don't know: documents, evidence, that's what he claimed...

(*The defense interrupts him.*)

DEFENSE – Is it possible that your brother never showed you the documents?

SALEMI – I wanted nothing to do with it. I had even resigned as town Councilman...

PROSECUTOR – (*Almost angrily*) – A few nights before he was killed, however, your brother stated that he had handed you a copy of this dossier. He said that if they killed him, justice would have the proof in hand...

(*Salemi tried two or three times to interrupt him with agitation.*)

SALEMI – That's not true, that's not true! I never had anything in my hands. Where's the sense in that...?

DEFENSE – And if you really had it in your possession, then what?

SALEMI – I would have handed it to the *carabinieri*!

PROSECUTOR – And is it not possible that your brother, before being killed, gave those documents to your mother...?

SALEMI – (*As if he did not understand right away*) – My mother? How could he...? My mother's dead...! No, no, completely out of the question.

PROSECUTOR – It could be among the things belonging to your mother. Did you ever look for it?

SALEMI – There is nothing left...! Even my mother's house was sold!

PROSECUTOR – You are excused!

(*The witness gets up but the Defense stops him with a hand gesture.*)

DEFENSE – Professor Salemi, was Attorney Emanuele Crupi one of the people accused of your brother's murder and then acquitted?

SALEMI – No! When my brother was killed, Mr. Crupi had been living in Rome for many months!

DEFENSE – Thank you!

(*As the witness goes off, he bows lightly.*)

DEFENSE – I ask that the witness remain in a secure room for further questioning...

(*There is a moment of silence and expectation.*)

PROSECUTOR – Defendant Emanuele Crupi!

(The silence is remarkable. The defendant stands and the other defendants in his row stand so he can pass. He comes forward very slowly. He is a tall, robust man, dressed in dark, with a black tie. He has gray hair, and he appears to be between 60 and 70 years of age. He is very controlled in his gestures, his tone of voice, and choice of words, and perhaps because of this he seems sure of himself. His slowness and air of sadness also give the imperceptible sensation that he is ill. After a gesture from the Prosecutor, he sits directly facing the Court.)

PROSECUTOR – Emanuele Crupi, 68 years old; a degree in law, farmer by profession?

CRUPI – Yes, Sir!

PROSECUTOR – According to the deeds, you are owner of some apartments, some agricultural machinery, heads of cattle, a building used for making cheese products and approximately 300 hectares of land, over 200 of which planted with citrus fruit trees and situated in the lower part of the Busambra river? Is this a correct assessment?

CRUPI – Yes, Sir, it's exact!

PROSECUTOR – There was a public project for the construction of a dam in the upper part of the Busambra, to collect the waters of the valley and irrigate 10,000 hectares of land. Were you familiar with this project?

CRUPI – Yes, Sir, I was familiar with it and I was against it! The dam would have flooded a large part of the valley and would have destroyed almost all the citrus groves.

PROSECUTOR – Your groves!

CRUPI – Mine also!

PROSECUTOR – What did you do, then?

CRUPI – I expressed my opposition!

PROSECUTOR – Is that all you did?

CRUPI – What else could I do?

PROSECUTOR – The dam project, however, failed. The funds were diverted to other public works in other regions. Building the dam would have created 10,000 hectares of fertile land. That land is a desert, instead...

CRUPI – I had to protect my groves. They belong to me, to my family, they cost me 50 years of sacrifices! It is not true that the water from the dam would have irrigated all of the 10,000 hectares. It would have cost 10 billion lire, the State would have built houses and stables for the peasants and they would have lived there, but after a year they would have sold their portion of land to come live again in town or emigrate. It has happened a number of times! They have burned mountains of money this way! If the water is not sufficient, if there is no electricity in the houses, if there are no streets, trees, farm machines, the land alone is not enough! The peasants want to live in town, go to the movies, watch TV, the young men want to be with women. Can't you see that the land is deserted...?

PROSECUTOR – Nevertheless, former Mayor Giuseppe Salemi believed in the need to build the dam...

CRUPI – Former Mayor Salemi was a passionate man in everything he did and said, but he was not sincere. He wasn't even a competent man.

PROSECUTOR – Is that why he was killed? Because he was incompetent or because he was too passionate?

CRUPI – Who can say? No one ever knew why he was killed. I think he had a lot of enemies.

PROSECUTOR – Union organizer Alicata also fought against the dam and he too was killed!

CRUPI – He too was a passionate man, but he was on a different level. Venero Alicata knew exactly what he wanted. He was a son of peasants and fought to help peasants. He had one fault, he did not understand that passion alone is not enough in life…

PROSECUTOR – What else do you need?

CRUPI – You need prudence, respect for others, patience and wisdom. These are the same qualities required of a person in your position, aren't they, Sir?

PROSECUTOR – You are accused of ordering the murder of Venero Alicata!

CRUPI – Yes, I know!

PROSECUTOR – You're also accused of causing the death of eight year old Mario Scibilia, killed at the same time. In addition, you're accused of ordering the killing of Carmelo Licitra and Inspector Ettore Florena, and finally, of being an accomplice in the massacre of eight *carabinieri* and soldiers.

CRUPI – Yes, Sir, I have been accused of twelve murders, criminal association and corruption. Nevertheless, I did not commit any of these crimes!

(*The Prosecutor calls out.*)

PROSECUTOR – Rosario Vacirca!

(*The defendant Vacirca rises.*)

PROSECUTOR – Defendant Rosario Vacirca confessed he killed Carmelo Licitra on Giovanni Savoca's order!

CRUPI – That is possible! It's possible, but I do not believe it. If Giovanni Savoca wanted to kill someone, he would have done it himself.

PROSECUTOR – You seem to have respect for him.

CRUPI – Yes, Sir! He is dead now, they killed him in an ambush, but I continue to have respect for him. He was a very loyal man.

PROSECUTOR – In his confession Rosario Vacirca said that Carmelo Licitra's murder was ordered by Giovanni Savoca, but that it was done in your behalf!

CRUPI – I don't know Rosario Vacirca. I never saw him before now! If that's what he says, he is insane!

PROSECUTOR – He confessed that Inspector Florena was also killed in your behalf!

CRUPI – He is insane!

(The Prosecutor calls out.)

PROSECUTOR – Defendant Luciano Verzì!

(Defendant Verzi rises.)

PROSECUTOR – Defendant Luciano Verzì confessed he killed inspector Florena on your order!

CRUPI – I don't know any of these men, but I read his confession! He denied it completely before the Magistrate. He also repeated it in this room: he confessed to avoid torture.

PROSECUTOR– Were you tortured during your questioning?

CRUPI – No, Sir, never! And in fact I never confessed! I'm an old man...they wouldn't have dared!

PROSECUTOR – You also claim you have not met defendant Verzì, is that right?

CRUPI – I have never seen him before now!

PROSECUTOR – Nevertheless, he said that it was through your recommendation that he obtained a Middle School diploma, in spite of the fact he was illiterate!

CRUPI – This too is possible! I made numberless recommendations for poor people. But I can barely remember ten names.

PROSECUTOR – The *carabinieri* escort have observed that when you leave your prison to get on the prisoner transport van Defendant Verzì greets you with extreme reverence...

CRUPI – I noticed this and I appreciate it! I am an old man and he behaves respectfully. But what can that mean? Mr. Prosecutor, you are an important and respectable person and if I chanced to meet you in the cafe I would feel obliged to greet you even if you don't remember my name… but does it mean that you are a criminal?

PROSECUTOR – And, naturally, you don't know defendant Filippo Giacalone either?

CRUPI – No, Sir!

PROSECUTOR – You have never seen or talked to him!?

CRUPI – I have never seen or talked to him!

(*Suddenly, in a loud voice, the Prosecutor turns to the defendants' cage)*

PROSECUTOR – Defendant Giacalone, you, on the other hand, said that you knew defendant Emanuele Crupi!

(*Defendant Giacalone rises and mutters something unintelligible.*)

DEFENSE – (*Courteously*) He said yes, that he knows him!

PROSECUTOR – Giacalone, you said you had gone over to ask Mr. Crupi for the party membership card. You went to his Palermo apartment.

(*Giacalone remains silent and motionless.*)

PROSECUTOR – Giacalone, listen to this question carefully! The car filled with dynamite that you abandoned in the middle of the street and whose explosion then killed the eight soldiers, was less than 300 yards from his apartment building. Was it moving in the direction of the building? You know the truth!

(*The defendant moves slowly, but no response is heard.*)

PROSECUTOR – Speak louder!

DEFENSE – Mr. Prosecutor, he said nothing. He didn't speak!

PROSECUTOR – Giacalone, I am being very patient with you. This is your only chance to save yourself. You have to show that other people gave you the car to drive from one part of town to another. You must tell us the name of the person who gave you the Giulietta... Answer me!

DEFENSE – He is not talking, Mr. Prosecutor! The defendant is ill...

PROSECUTOR – (*Violently.*) You are a madman, Giacalone! You are putting the weight of eight murders on your head

(*He makes and angry gesture and yells.*)

Imbecile, don't you have a family? Don't you love your children?

DEFENSE – (*Rises up in a loud voice.*) This is a moral blackmail. You are forcing that poor man to lie.

(*The Prosecutor's voice overpowers the defense lawyer's.*)

PROSECUTOR – I could consider this a contempt offense...

DEFENSE – It's my duty to defend this helpless man from abuse.

PROSECUTOR – I am simply asking the defendant confess the whole truth now! Because he knows the truth...

(*The Defense violently interrupts him again.*)

DEFENSE – You are asking him to invent a confession in exchange for your mercy... you are asking him to commit perjury...

PROSECUTOR – This too is a contempt offense!

DEFENSE – (*Making an effort to keep calm*) Let's be calm, let's not lose the perspective on words. (*He rises.*) It is useless anyway… Giacalone... you may sit down again.

(*He looks at the Prosecutor silently for a moment with a kind of strange benevolence.*)

The fact is, Mr. Prosecutor, that you have a plan... I realized it from the beginning. No need to be upset… You pinned the success of the prosecution on four precise elements... four infallible proofs. In your opinion, only one of these proofs is sufficient to prove the rest. First proof: you called professor Salemi hoping to get the dossier written by his brother, the Mayor, before being killed. That dossier supposedly contained the names of the murderers… But, Mr. Salemi no longer has the documents, he never had them…it was surely a hoax… Second proof: You tried to bring here Mrs. Scibilia, the mother of the child killed with union organizer Alicata. A wretched human wreck! You were hoping that she had seen the murderer's face... But she remembers nothing, she's ill, insane, she nearly died and the doctors forbade you to bring her in the Courtroom...I know!...The third proof was to be Giacalone: this man whom you yourself described as a habitual thief, a compulsive liar suffering delusions, a vice-ridden deserter, no longer capable of rehabilitation. Nevertheless, you still hope to get his clamorous confession on the authors of the massacre… But Giacalone can't speak for the simple fact that he knows nothing; he has become a terror-stricken, little animal by things he cannot even understand… Fourth proof... and you really think you have this one in your grasp... defendant Rosario Vacirca's confession, which compromises all the other defendants. But when he is called to testify, I will show you that he is truly insane! There...

(*He smiles understandingly*)

I understand your persistence… how should I characterize it?… your passionate and evident anger when you realize one of these proofs has failed. But it really gives the impression you want to terrify that poor Giacalone.

PROSECUTOR – He knows the truth and I will get him to admit it no matter what it costs. Nevertheless, in spite of the defendant's denial, Giacalone has already confessed that he had met Mr. Crupi in person…

(During this time, defendant Crupi has remained seated, without moving and without turning around. His voice suddenly interrupts the proceedings.)

Mr. Prosecutor, if I may, during the period referred to by that fellow Giacalone, that is, after the elections, from that area there were about 3,000 new applications for membership in the party. It's possible that he really came to my house…

PROSECUTOR – But you have no recollection of him?

CRUPI – How can I remember him? There were hundreds of people…Many came to me by mistake…

PROSECUTOR – What do you mean, by mistake?

CRUPI – I mean that I was not engaged in any political activity. I had no official role and I have never been a candidate in any election.

PROSECUTOR – You had no political power! Yet you were able to get a Middle School diploma for illiterates…

CRUPI – I admit it. But if making recommendations were a crime, then you'd have to jail half Italy. Nothing would work any more!

PROSECUTOR – You had no political power, yet you were able to stop the building of a dam, to name doctors to the town's Medical Care Programs, select employees for the welfare agencies and banks… The records state that you were able to orchestrate at will most of the political events in your province.

CRUPI – That's an exaggeration. I am honored, however, to have the friendship of people who in turn can exercise influence over political life. Someone must exercise influence in behalf of the citizens, otherwise, it is no longer politics…

PROSECUTOR – You were able to summon, that is, you were able to swing a block of thirty thousand votes…

CRUPI – I don't know if they were thirty or thirty thousand, but I have done favors for many people in my life. I am unable to say no to anyone who comes to me for something. That's my shortcoming. I am a whore at heart. But even this is not a crime. Mr. Prosecutor, I stand accused of twelve murders and I said I did not know any of the murdered people. What does all the rest matter?

PROSECUTOR – Do you really believe the rest has nothing to do with you?

CRUPI – I don't think so, Sir. Surely if those twelve men were murdered, there must have been a motive for killing them. Nothing ever happens without a motive... At any rate, do you want me to give you my honest opinion of those men? Mayor Giuseppe Salemi was a failure in his profession as a physician and had reached for political office as his only chance to save himself. He was an ignorant, hardheaded and violent person who went knocking on people's door to ask for votes. He owed money to half the town, he was even filthy in his body; and he was a bully. Once he repeatedly kicked a municipal guard in his office. He wanted to run for Parliament. Everything he did and said had this objective. There were probably a thousand people who had an interest in killing him. He was a poor man who mistook his stupidity for passion and he was able to convince many other imbeciles. He harmed people... But Inspector Florena did more harm because he was not stupid...Inspector Florena was greedy, vicious, corrupt, but he was also cunning and patient, that is, he was willing to sell his authority at a high price, but not to everyone. He left no trace of his dishonesty. On the other hand, he had collected evidence against everyone who dealt with him. He had them all in his hands. Now neither I nor you know who these people were. So how can you find out who among them killed him?

PROSECUTOR – You said nothing about Alicata, the union organizer!

CRUPI – I know nothing about him. A man who fought and now is dead.

PROSECUTOR – (*Calling toward the cage*) Amedeo Barresi, please, stand up! What's your opinion of Amedeo Barresi who stands accused of fourteen murders?

CRUPI – What opinion should I have? He is alive.

PROSECUTOR – You have opinions about men only when they're dead?

CRUPI – Of course not. I meant that we were talking only about dead people. I never heard mention of the man you're showing me. I saw him in this room for the first time and I admit he is exactly as the papers described him: young and elegant, with black glasses like a movie star. I am not impressed!

(*There's mumbling in the cage. Amedeo Barresi looks around smiling.*)

PROSECUTOR – Nevertheless, you stand accused of committing twelve murders in a struggle against this man...

CRUPI – I repeat, I am not impressed... Allegedly I had twelve people killed whom I did not know in a struggle against a man I had never seen in my life! Does that make any sense?

PROSECUTOR – He had killed one of your loyal men before the door to your house, leaving him there like a bloody hulk. It was a challenge!

He used your territory to smuggle goods, bought up the building zones you had tried to secure…

(*The defendant interrupts him.*)

CRUPI – "He also had bribed the Inspector and had become too friendly with the politicians…" Yes, Sir, I read all these things in the transcripts of the pretrial questioning, but he does not strike me as a capable man… I don't believe it. I never heard his name mentioned…

(*Amedeo Barresi continues to smile and then sits down.*)

PROSECUTOR – But you knew Inspector Florena personally, didn't you?

CRUPI – Yes, Sir. I had met him several times on official ceremonies. Once he graciously helped me renew my permit to carry arms. He was corrupt, but gracious…

PROSECUTOR – And you also had occasions to go to his house...

CRUPI – Yes, Sir, twice, on account of that permit and to ask him to speed up the release of an acquaintance.

PROSECUTOR – Did you succeed?

CRUPI – Yes, Sir. It was his right! Both times inspector Florena was gracious and understanding. He knew how to treat people…He had only one shortcoming: he was too submissive with his wife, but he was right… she was a very beautiful and sweet woman. The inspector was crazy about her…

PROSECUTOR – Very romantic, indeed! From what you just said you don't seem too unhappy about inspector Florena's death!

CRUPI – To tell the truth, when I learned from the papers that he had been killed, I thought that it was something in the natural order of things. I thought the same thing when they came to tell me that Mayor Salemi had been killed in the middle of the square. The death of a stupid or cowardly man does not make me unhappy.

PROSECUTOR – You show great disdain for the lives of others… You're surrounded by a pack of murderers, yet you're talking as if your way of life were justified by some ideal…

CRUPI – This too is a word that can mean many things and nothing. You are fighting to send these people to prison for life and they to save themselves. Both are ideals…

PROSECUTOR – I was asking you about your ideal…

CRUPI – I don't know if you can call it an ideal. I do believe in something, but it's difficult to explain, that is, I can't prove it: it's only a kind of instinct, that's all… Survival after death, I am convinced, is achieved only by those souls who have lived with great passion, who have felt all the passions of life, sorrow, love, even violence and murder, defending that life in every way with brutal fierceness.... No moment in their lives has not been fed by their passion, that very life nurtured and nourished inside their breasts without ever tiring for a moment...even though life may end in a second: an act of rebellion, a sacrifice in the midst of the battle...

(*He pauses for a moment.*)

Mr. Prosecutor, am I to return to my seat ?

(*After the prosecutor nods, he gets up, bowing imperceptibly before the Court, and heads for the defendants' bench. Meanwhile the Prosecutor calls out.*)

PROSECUTOR – I call witness Mario...

(*From the back of the room Rosalia Alicata's scream interrupts him.*)

ROSALIA – You're letting him go just like that? Instead of keeping him there until he told you who killed my son?

PROSECUTOR – Rosalia Alicata, keep quiet!

(*Suddenly the Defense Attorney jumps up with anger in his voice.*)

DEFENSE – No, do come forward, Rosalia Alicata! Come forward and listen... I respect your desperation, but you are talking and crying as if you were the only mother on the face of this earth. In fact, outside this room, even behind that very cage there are countless black-veiled mothers weeping. Come forward once and for all, for I will not let you frustrate the course of justice.

(*Rosalia Alicata comes forward slowly, silently, with her eyes fixed on the Defense Attorney who continues to speak in a loud voice.*)

DEFENSE – Rosalia Alicata, you stated before the *carabinieri* that your son was violently opposed to Mr. Crupi, that he led peasants to occupy his lands, and organized migrant workers to demonstrate against the building of the dam...

ROSALIA – (*With the same violent tone*) So what? Isn't it true?

DEFENSE – Of course, it's true! Your son was arrested three times for violence, inciting a riot, defamation, and breaking and entering.

ROSALIA – They could not fight him any other way. That's why they persecuted him. They burned his car, they broke his arm... You don't know what my son was like, the courage he had, the way he got people to follow him...

DEFENSE – We know what your son was, he went around with many different women.. . once a foreign megalomaniac, another time a whore...

ROSALIA – Women lay down for him, they pulled him down on them.

DEFENSE – That's your business…

ROSALIA – (*Always cutting him off.*) And so?

DEFENSE – And so, in front of the *carabinieri*, you stated that Emanuele Crupi had had your son killed, he could not fight him any other way, so he had him killed. Is that true or not? But here in the Courtroom, on the other hand, you said that it had been Barresi who had had him killed. You said that you had the evidence...

ROSALIA – I said what I knew.

DEFENSE – (*Insisting*) You said it was Barresi who had threatened to kill him! You said it and screamed it in front of everyone. So then, Rosalia Alicata, you must explain how it's possible for Emanuele Crupi to have killed your son now, if you stated before that Amedeo Barresi had killed him.

ROSALIA – These are words...

(*But the Defense Attorney insists.*)

DEFENSE – Haven't you heard what is being said in this trial? Emanuele Crupi and Amedeo Barresi are mortal enemies… or do you want to change the direction of this case?

(*Finally Rosalia Alicata, nearly choking on her anger, screams.*)

ROSALIA – Am I supposed to tell you who killed Venero Alicata? You must bring him here before me, covered with gangrene and with his eyes ripped out, and I want to see him die before me... seven days and seven nights of agony before dying...I want to see his mother here and see how she weeps.

DEFENSE – You want a victim for your sorrow, no matter what it costs...

(*Rosalia Alicata lets out a cry, a desperate gesture toward the Court.*)

ROSALIA – Honorable Judges, you must give me justice... Do you know what it means for a woman to have only one son? She puts all pleasure and sorrow in him… When he's young she feels like putting him back inside her womb to keep him warm and away from harm. Instead she watches him grow up and become a man… She has nothing else in her life except that one son...

PROSECUTOR – Rosalia Alicata...!

ROSALIA – (*With a heart-rending voice*) You must listen to me...

(But her voice dies out as a moan.)

and then she sees him dead... *(She screams)*... They were all in it ...all together to murder him... and you want to make a fool of me...

PROSECUTOR – Rosalia Alicata...!

ROSALIA – You're good with words...I am only an ignorant peasant, but I am not taking back a single word, you must nail me first inside a coffin. They even came to my house to offer me five million lire, to drop the charges. They refused to tell me who they were... Emanuele Crupi, you sent them, didn't you? Five million lire soaked in blood... you wanted to buy Rosalia Alicata's conscience with that... If my son had lived...with all your arrogance... he would have crushed your head against the rocks. Or maybe it was you who sent those men, Amedeo Barresi. Did that money belong to you...? You dirty, filthy, miserable man... You are not even worth five cents...

(A carabiniere approaches her, taking her by the arm, but Rosalia Alicata frees herself with a gesture. She recoils shuddering.)

ROSALIA – Don't put your hands on me!

(Without even turning to face the Court she slowly starts walking towards the back. She sits down and remains motionless, while the prosecutor calls out.)

PROSECUTOR – I call witness Mario Zaccaria!

(The witness quickly approaches from the left. He is about 40 years old, normal height, dressed in gray with unmistakable upper class elegance. He looks at no one, not even the Prosecutor or the defendants and proceeds to sit quietly before the Court. He does not show any awkwardness or emotion.)

PROSECUTOR – Mario Zaccaria, 45 years of age, Member of Parliament?

ZACCARIA – Yes!

PROSECUTOR – Forgive us for making you come to this courtroom, but it was essential.

ZACCARIA – It was my duty!

PROSECUTOR – Before being elected to Parliament, what profession did you practice?

ZACCARIA – I continue to practice law even now. Why shouldn't I?

PROSECUTOR – Can you tell us how many votes you received in the election?

ZACCARIA – Certainly! Fifty-two thousand votes! Forgive me, but may I ask you the purpose of such a question? Since I was called as a witness, I thought I had to answer specific questions only regarding the trial.

PROSECUTOR – That's true! Let me then ask you a more precise question. Was Emanuele Crupi a member of the organizing committee of your election campaign?

ZACCARIA – Yes, he was a member! He presided over the committee that organized the election campaign in the province...

PROSECUTOR – Can you be more specific?

ZACCARIA – Certainly: there were two election committees, the first was in charge of the organization of the election in the cities, that is, in the province capitals, the second was in charge of all the other towns in the provinces. Mr. Crupi presided over the second committee.

PROSECUTOR – What does an election organization do?

ZACCARIA – It identifies and gains votes for the party and for the candidate. It organizes speeches, conferences, produces publicity for billboards, radio spots...

PROSECUTOR – Pardon me; among the tasks of the election committee to get votes, is there a place for personal lobbying for the votes of private individuals, to persuade individual voters?

ZACCARIA – Sometimes, naturally...

PROSECUTOR – Well, is such a technique more fruitful... rather... how can I put it? Does it get better results in a large city, or in small province towns where everyone knows one another?

(*The witness remains silent for a second.*)

ZACCARIA – In the province towns, obviously!

PROSECUTOR – Now I have to go back to my clumsy question about the votes you received. A more precise question, nevertheless: do you recall how many votes you received in the capital city and how many in the towns of the province?

ZACCARIA – I can't give you precise figures...

PROSECUTOR – Approximate figures will do...

ZACCARIA – I think... perhaps seven thousand votes in the capital and forty-five thousand in the province.

PROSECUTOR – So, you received most of your votes from the districts where the election campaign was chaired by Mr. Emanuele Crupi?

ZACCARIA – That is obvious!

(*The Defense raises his hand.*)

DEFENSE – Pardon me, Mr. Zaccaria, if my question may also appear superfluous! Do you believe that without Emanuele Crupi's collaboration, the election results would have been different? I mean: would you have received fewer or more votes?

ZACCARIA – I don't think I can answer that question. I have no data on which to base a reply. Mr. Crupi was one of hundreds of people who contributed to my election. I am proud to say, however, that I, myself, am most responsible for the esteem in which people hold my person...

PROSECUTOR – No one is trying to question that...

ZACCARIA – Nevertheless, the questions you are asking strike me as somewhat odd...

PROSECUTOR – True. In reality, they may seem odd, but I ask you to forgive me for them and for those I still need to ask you regarding another individual...

(A large group photo is projected onto the back wall.)

PROSECUTOR – Do you recognize this photo?

ZACCARIA – Of course! I can even tell you the day when it was taken: the last day of the election campaign, in April, two years ago.

PROSECUTOR – Then, you can probably recognize the people next to you..?

ZACCARIA – One by one! From the left, the party's Regional Secretary, La Rosa, Deputy Benfi...

(The Prosecutor interrupts him.)

PROSECUTOR – The man on your left, marked with a white cross. Do you recognize him?

ZACCARIA – Of course. Amedeo Barresi!

(The picture quickly focuses on the face of the Deputy making a speech and on Barresi's face slightly in the background.)

PROSECUTOR – Can you recognize him inside the cell? Will you look...

ZACCARIA – No need! I saw him when I came in! The second from the left, on top, the one with dark glasses.

PROSECUTOR – The photo you are looking at was found in Barresi's wallet when he was arrested. Also your phone number was found in Defendant Barresi's agenda. Mr. Barresi finally admitted that he had written three checks to you for charity. What is this man to you? An acquaintance, a friend?

ZACCARIA – Mr. Prosecutor, I would like you to define your concept of "friend" first.

PROSECUTOR – What can I say? A friend is a person who is close to us, whose ideas and habits we share, from whom we accept advice and recommendations, with whom we have an arrangement for mutual protection.

DEFENSE – I object! This is a string of insinuations.

PROSECUTOR – So, let the Defense give a definition of friendship, or else suggest a way to learn from the Deputy, who is so scrupulous in using the right terminology, what his real relationship with defendant Barresi was.

ZACCARIA – He was not a friend of mine!

PROSECUTOR – That means that he was not a person from whom you accepted important advice or to whom your powerful protection did not extend?

ZACCARIA – Please, explain what you mean by "powerful protection"?

PROSECUTOR – Mr. Zaccaria, we are discussing words that have no meaning! The Court wants to know how it was possible for Amedeo Barresi to give you three checks for charity, stand on the dais with you at a political rally, carry your picture and phone number in his wallet. In a word, if you knew him. You are reacting as though we are trying to violate your private personality. We simply want to know who defendant Barresi was and how much political influence he had…

ZACCARIA – I knew him. It's undeniable.

PROSECUTOR – How did you know him? He is regarded as a criminal. He has been accused of twelve murders, fraud, usury, corruption, smuggling and making false statements.

ZACCARIA – I did not know him in that light. I meet hundreds of people every day.

PROSECUTOR – Under what light did you know him? What was he, in your opinion?

ZACCARIA – How can you define a person?

PROSECUTOR – Try to do it, please!

ZACCARIA – He was a very well-mannered man, eager to be of service. Will you accept this as a definition? He was always very loyal…

PROSECUTOR – What else?

ZACCARIA – He was polite! And he certainly was also very useful…

PROSECUTOR – Useful in what way? The records clearly show that you accepted a few of his recommendations. You also recommended to private and public agencies people that Barresi had recommended… Why?

ZACCARIA – I always consider names given to me by those who have been politically close to me. All voters have the right to make requests and send advisory notes to a Member of Parliament and he has the right to consider them.

PROSECUTOR – I don't want to know how you behave with your voters. I want to know a specific fact. Why did you act on Amedeo Barresi's advisory notes?

ZACCARIA – Forgive me, Mr. Prosecutor, but this time you're the one discussing meaningless words... Clearly, I meant to compensate him for his loyalty.

PROSECUTOR – What, may I ask, was the most concrete manifestation of this loyalty?

ZACCARIA – He got votes for me, Mr. Prosecutor, if that's what you wanted to know! He got votes for me and therefore I had to presume that he and I shared the same political ideas. I considered it my duty to trust him.

PROSECUTOR – So, is this the reason why you accepted his recommendations?

ZACCARIA – They were advisory notes. That's all. I repeat! Advisory notes that any voter has the right to submit. It's possible that, following my conscience, I acted on some of them. Let me answer a question you will surely ask me. Who was I supposed to support, instead, my political adversaries?

PROSECUTOR – All of this is not very ethical.

ZACCARIA – It's only a thing made by men and thus quite human. I am tempted, for the third time, to ask you what you mean by ethical... or maybe you want to teach me that things happen differently? Would you swear to me that no magistrate, when he took the competition examination to enter the profession, has ever benefited from a politician's recommendation? Had I not recommended those who had given me their votes, those positions and privileges would have gone to the people recommended by my political adversaries.

PROSECUTOR – This is a rather shabby problem!

ZACCARIA – Your questions have brought the whole discussion to this shabby level.

PROSECUTOR – I have the right to ask necessary questions. And I have the right to require you to respect Justice.

ZACCARIA – Not even Justice has the right to contaminate a witness with its suspicions. It must discuss specific facts and nothing more. Two plus two equals four!... I knew Barresi, as I have known thousands of other voters, and Barresi knew me, as he probably knows ten other Members of Parliament.

(There is a moment of silence.)

DEFENSE – Allow me to bother you, Mr. Zaccaria, with a few simple questions: you stated that Amadeo Barresi obtained votes for you... Did he also preside over an election committee?

ZACCARIA – No!

DEFENSE – Did he have a political following? Make speeches?

ZACCARIA – No!

DEFENSE – Please tell me with absolute certainty the number of votes you could count on from Amedeo Barresi! Not a supposition, please, but an absolutely certain figure: how many votes?

ZACCARIA – Only one, his alone.

DEFENSE – And how can you be certain, absolutely certain, of his vote?

ZACCARIA – You're right! Not even his!

DEFENSE – You've been very kind...

(*The witness bows to the Court and leaves. A voice breaks the silence from the cage.*)

VOICE – Mr. President, Filippo Giacalone is not well!

ANOTHER VOICE – He was crying....

(*A moment of silence.*)

PROSECUTOR – Defendant Giacalone!

(*Giacalone rises to his feet. He has a desperate look on his face.*)

PROSECUTOR – What's wrong with you, Giacalone ?

(*Giacalone remains silent, immobile.*)

VOICE – He was moaning, he said he was in pain…

PROSECUTOR – Spit it out, Giacalone, what's wrong?

(*Giacalone is silent. He simply stares unmoving with a look of desperation on his face.*)

PROSECUTOR – Did they threaten you again, or do you really feel sick?

(*Giacalone does not answer.*)

PROSECUTOR – Take your seat again!

(*Giacalone takes his seat among the others, remaining frozen.*)

PROSECUTOR – I propose that the Court listen to the three following witnesses: Prof. Giovanni Aulino, Dr. Eugenio Saluzzo, and Dr. Giacomo Interlandi.

(The three witnesses appear from the left, almost single file. Three well-to-do people. A nod from the Prosecutor and they come forward together to face the Court.)

FIRST WITNESS – Prof. Giovanni Aulino, son of the late Girolamo, 49 years old, Principal at the Garibaldi Intermediate School.

SECOND WITNESS – Dr. Eugene Saluzzo, 41 years old, Vice-collector of direct taxes!

THIRD WITNESS – Dr. Giacomo Interlandi, 51 years old, Vice-Police Chief!

PROSECUTOR – Prof. Aulino, three years ago, in June, you presided over the exam committee for intermediate licenses! Is that correct?

AULINO – Yes, Sir! I remember that I had been very ill that year and heavy-heartedly accepted the position. In fact, I had asked to be exonerated but…

PROSECUTOR – *(Interrupting him)* In that session one of the candidates, Luciano Verzì, passed the exams in spite of the fact he was illiterate. Can you explain how that happened?

(The witness shrugs his shoulder and then tries to concentrate.)

PROSECUTOR – You were the president of that Committee. I asked you to explain how it happened?

AULINO – He probably had a copy of the written essays and of the math problem. I cannot give you an explanation; it could have been an error...

PROSECUTOR – In other words, a scam?

AULINO – I meant an error on the part of the Committee.

PROSECUTOR – Do you mean to say that a man who can't read or write comes before an Examining Committee and by mistake passes both the written and oral exams? What kind of error?

(The witness makes a hesitant gesture with his hand, opens his mouth as if to speak but does not say anything. The Prosecutor turns to the other witness.)

PROSECUTOR – Dr. Interlandi, Police Headquarters, in fact, your own office, received an anonymous complaint regarding High School diplomas that were being handed out to illiterates… But we just learned of it!

INTERLANDI – As a matter of fact, there was a complaint. But we receive two hundred anonymous complaints a month, many of which are implausible.

PROSECUTOR – Was this report regarded as implausible? Wasn't there an investigation?

INTERLANDI – We questioned the President of the Committee…! But nothing came of it.

PROSECUTOR – What do you mean, "nothing came of it"?

INTERLANDI – The President confirmed that there had been no irregularities. He had the records… After all, it was his responsibility…

AULINO – I confirmed only that I signed the records regularly, that's all! What was I supposed to do? Let's not change the truth!

INTERLANDI – (*Reacting in kind*) You said that the exams had been conducted with absolute normality…you guaranteed it.

AULINO – I was talking about the records…

(*The Prosecutor curtly interrupts and turns to Interlandi.*)

PROSECUTOR – But weren't these illiterates called in for questioning?

(*Witness Interlandi leans forward as if to indicate he did not understand the question.*)

INTERLANDI – Sorry, Your Honor…

PROSECUTOR – (*Raising his voice*) Were these illiterates ever brought in for questioning? How difficult is it to see if a man can't read or write?

INTERLANDI – We could not find them, your Honor. We looked for them, some had even left the country. Often these minor cases are assigned to a single agent… then sometimes he gets transferred…

PROSECUTOR – What do you consider, then, an important case? Is a one hundred million lire a year tax evasion, for example, an important case?

INTERLANDI – I did not understand…

PROSECUTOR – (*Raising his voice again*) Let me give you an example: Amedeo Barresi, owns thirty apartments, lots in building zones and two hotels, and for the last eight years he has been paying taxes on barely three million lire of declared income. Did you receive any anonymous complaints about this too?

INTERLANDI – Verifying income is a responsibility of the provincial office… We have no initiative in that area…

PROSECUTOR – (*Turning to the third witness.*) That is to say, Dr. Saluzzo, that income verification is your responsibility…

SALUZZO – (*Losing his composure.*) What do you mean, my responsibility? The office relies first of all on the contributor's declaration…

PROSECUTOR – But a contributor can also make a false declaration. What do you do then?

SALUZZO – We have the means to investigate, we can order audits and inspections.

PROSECUTOR – Are you ever subjected to influences or intimidations?

SALUZZO – Of course, contributors fight against the fiscal authority…

PROSECUTOR – (*Harshly*) Answer the question correctly.

AULINO – (*Nervously*) I mean to say that contributors fight, I mean, in the sense that everyone is looking for influences and recommendations… but our office rejects them. They then look for other avenues…

PROSECUTOR – What avenues?

SALUZZO – They try to hide, to disguise themselves.

PROSECUTOR – But even in extreme cases you have the means to unmask them, nail them against reality, don't you?

SALUZZO – A perfect control is not possible, our personnel is inadequate…

PROSECUTOR – Do you or don't you have the means?

(*The witness opens and closes his eyelids frightened.*)

SALUZZO – Yes, Sir!

PROSECUTOR – What means? Let's hear them!

SALUZZO – The police, the *carabinieri* also…

INTERLANDI – (*Interrupting him.*) But you are the one who is supposed to initiate the actions, to bring charges…

SALUZZO – We start the procedures, but months and years pass before getting any results…

INTERLANDI – (*Rebelling.*) Our office does what it can…Often however, the dossiers received collect dust… that's true!

SALUZZO – I can say, however, that that is not true! I can document, on the other hand, attempts by known authorities to let certain investigations decant…

PROSECUTOR – Decant? How?

SALUZZO – By not touching them, letting them sink to the bottom… But we've always thwarted such attempts…

PROSECUTOR – And how does one let an investigation decant? Be clear!

SALUZZO – Some times a required certificate or a document or the results of a police investigation, never arrives.

PROSECUTOR – (*To Interlandi*) Has your office ever received a request to audit Amedeo Barresi?

INTERLANDI – Yes, Sir, once… but it was quickly blocked. The dossier was withdrawn…

SALUZZO – (*With an angry outburst.*) That is false! The dossier needed to be completed. In fact, it was returned again so the investigation could continue.

INTERLANDI – (*Angrily too.*) After two years! Try and say that this too is false!

SALUZZO – But it has never been given back…The whole fiscal procedure was paralyzed!

INTERLANDI – It takes time!

PROSECUTOR – It takes time, it always takes time… Dr. Interlandi, how long does it take to find out that a citizen has a record?

INTERLANDI – What do you mean? What kind of record?

PROSECUTOR – (*Curtly*) According to the records, defendant Luciano Verzì, convicted of murder and crimes against property, had a regular license to carry a gun, and defendant Amedeo Barresi, convicted nine times for acts of violence, had a legal permit to carry weapons too. In spite of the fact that he had a record and had been condemned to confinement, he obtained a regular passport…another twenty ex-convicts in this Court accused of murder, violence, and criminal associations all possessed the right to carry weapons. How can it happen that the Police Department allows very dangerous individuals to walk around with guns?

(*The witness is immobile for a few seconds as though reflecting on the question. He closes his eyes half way then leans slightly forward.*)

INTERLANDI – Forgive me, I did not hear the question exactly.

PROSECUTOR – You heard it! Explain how an ex-convict can obtain a license to carry a gun?

INTERLANDI – Your honor, we record twenty thousand requests for renewals or licenses to carry weapons. For each one we must conduct a detailed investigation, we have to check the penal records, find information…

PROSECUTOR – And do you do it?

INTERLANDI – In reality, I left the administrative section a year ago, I have taken part in numerous police actions, one of which involved even gunfire …

PROSECUTOR – (*Harshly*) Answer only the question!

INTERLANDI – Yes, Sir. We always order the investigations. It can happen, however, that there are false documents, erroneous data, we have to continuously update twenty thousand dossiers… A mistake is possible…

PROSECUTOR – And if I were to ask you what mistake allowed you to give a gun permit to convicted criminals like Luciano Verzì or Amedeo Barresi, could you be specific?

(The witness smiles faintly and leans forward again as if he did not understand.)

INTERLANDI – Excuse me, I did not understand *(as though he suddenly understood)* No, Sir! Not possible. Sometimes…

PROSECUTOR – Sometimes?

INTERLANDI – Sometimes, an ex-convict can be favored for the sake of opportunity, for services rendered …

PROSECUTOR – Services rendered to whom?

INTERLANDI – To our office, I mean to State Authorities…

PROSECUTOR – Can you tell us what possible services were rendered by Luciano Verzì or Amedeo Barresi?

INTERLANDI – I have never met the defendants… They may have been informants. We would have to investigate…

(The prosecutor turns to the witness Saluzzo.)

PROSECUTOR – You have never met Emanuele Crupi or Amedeo Barresi either, have you?

SALUZZO – No, Sir. Thousands of fiscal dossiers cross my desk.

(The Prosecutor to witness Aulino.)

PROSECUTOR – You also have never met any of the illiterates who received a Middle School diploma. Is that so?

AULINO – I don't remember their names any more.

PROSECUTOR – You have never been threatened…or offered any bribes?

AULINO – *(Gets confused)* Perhaps some of my colleagues…for myself, no! I had been very ill, as I said before. My involvement was limited to simply signing the transcripts placed before me…

PROSECUTOR – Nevertheless, a few months after that session of exams you obtained the transfer to Palermo. You had been asking for it for five years without success, but you were not eligible for it, you did not possess the right qualifications…

AULINO – My children were attending the university…I am the recipient of a Gold Medal for Public Education

PROSECUTOR – You may leave!

AULINO – I am also a veteran…

PROSECUTOR – You may all leave!

(The three witnesses rapidly leave without looking at one another. While they are getting farther away, the calm voice of the Defense Attorney.)

DEFENSE – Mr. Prosecutor, I trust you appreciated my discretion. I refrained from questioning your three witnesses. I know there's a fourth, the child of one of the men killed....

PROSECUTOR – (*Calls out.*) Salvatore Licitra!

DEFENSE – (*Continuing.*) I also know that he is a boy, but I cannot promise to listen to him with the same benevolence....

(*A boy about ten years old steps forward, dressed a bit gawkily, with a little black overcoat. At first, he halts at the center, soon after he steps forward. He stands with his arms along his sides, he looks at the ceiling a few times, squinting a bit, that is, without moving his head.*)

PROSECUTOR – What's your name?

TOTI – Salvatore Licitra.

PROSECUTOR – They also call you Toti?

TOTI – Yes, Sir!

PROSECUTOR – How old are you?

TOTI – Ten years old.

PROSECUTOR – Listen, Toti! Listen to me carefully! You told the *carabinieri* that one day, while you were in the countryside with your father, a car with several men stopped near you. Do you remember this?

TOTI – Yes, Sir!

PROSECUTOR – One of the men got out of the car and said something to you and your father. Do you recall what he said?

TOTI – Yes, Sir. He told my father: "Carmelo Licitra, why don't you start dressing your little boy in black?" He even patted me on my head and said: "Poor boy!"

PROSECUTOR – Just "poor boy"?

TOTI – "Poor boy! He will look so pale, dressed in black!"

PROSECUTOR – What did your father answer?

TOTI – Nothing! The man returned to his car and they left. My father said they were joking, then he made me sit on the motorcycle behind him and we left....

PROSECUTOR – And what happened then? Did your father explain who the men were? Did you ever see them again?

TOTI – No, Sir! My father died!

PROSECUTOR – Do you know how your father died?

TOTI – Yes, Sir. They shot him one night in an ambush.

PROSECUTOR – Listen, Toti! Do you remember what he looked like, the man who got out of the car to speak to your father?

TOTI – He was old, big, with no hair, he had an overcoat and a scarf…

PROSECUTOR – And the other men in the car with him.... do you remember what they looked like?

TOTI – The one who drove the car was young! The other was old too....

PROSECUTOR – Try to describe him, tell us what he looked like.

TOTI – An old man, dressed in a black overcoat and a hat!

PROSECUTOR – Listen, Toti, if I showed you that man, would you recognize him!

TOTI – Of course, I would!

PROSECUTOR – (*In a loud voice*): Defendant Emanuele Crupi!

(*While defendant Crupi slowly comes forward, the Prosecutor continues to address the boy.*)

PROSECUTOR – Do you go to school?

TOTI – Not anymore! I went up to the third grade!

PROSECUTOR – And what do you do now?

TOTI – I work! I pick olives, collect manure, water the animals and at night I play with my friends!

(*While talking he looks at defendant Crupi who is coming forward. He now stares at him in silence.*)

CRUPI – What a good-looking boy! What's your name?

TOTI – Toti!

CRUPI – And smart, too, Toti!

TOTI – Smart, why? Because they killed my father?

CRUPI – What are you saying, sweet boy! You are good-looking and smart because you are male! Do you have your "little pistol," Toti? You see, it's important to have a "little pistol".

PROSECUTOR – Look at him closely, Toti! Do you recognize him?

TOTI – Yes, Sir. It's him!

PROSECUTOR – Are you sure it's him? Can you be wrong?

TOTI – No, Sir. I am not wrong.

PROSECUTOR – Does the Defense have anything to ask this boy?

DEFENSE – No, Mr. Prosecutor. I request, however, that the minor, Salvatore Licitra, remain here in Courtroom.

(*While the boy, a bit hesitantly, approaches the back of the room and sits on a bench near the defendants' cage, the Defense continues.*)

DEFENSE – But I would like to ask a question that you will surely ask the defendant: Mr. Crupi, does what the boy said correspond to the truth?

CRUPI – Yes, Sir, it's true! I was in the car when Giovanni Savoca spoke with Carmelo Licitra and the boy…

(*He pauses briefly and then leans on his cane.*)

Excuse me, Mr. Prosecutor, if I speak slowly, but I did not feel well last night. This old carcass does not function anymore! Every so often I need to catch my breath.

PROSECUTOR – You can continue your deposition sitting down.

(*The defendant sits down slowly.*)

CRUPI – Thank you, Mr. Prosecutor. You're very gracious.

PROSECUTOR – You have the right to a chair during the deposition....

CRUPI – That means the law is very gracious, too...

(*He concentrates for a moment.*)

Yes, indeed, I was in the car when Giovanni Savoca spoke those words to Carmelo Licitra. I heard them perfectly, they were exactly as the boy recalled them. I have already said it: it's possible that Giovanni Savoca had Carmelo Licitra killed …If he did, I am sure he killed him with his own hands... But only the two of them could say what really happened and why they fought like that! But, at this point, they are both dead!

PROSECUTOR – Defendant Crupi, do you know that....

CRUPI – (*Interrupting him*): Yes, Sir, I know... the Prosecution claims that Giovanni Savoca killed Carmelo Licitra at my request, but that is not true... You can't prove it. The Prosecution claims many things... that I had Carmelo Licitra killed, that I had Inspector Florena killed...

PROSECUTOR – We will do all it takes to prove it… to the end.

CRUPI – I realize, Mr. Prosecutor that if I were in your place, wearing that gown, and here I saw a man like me, I would fight against him exactly as you are doing! I am perfectly aware that everything is against me... the dam that wasn't built, the thirty thousand votes that I control…these things convince you that I am guilty of those twelve homicides! The motives are certainly there... Everything seems possible, that I, in fact, could be the man who ordered those murders. The only thing is you have no proof. The only people who could have testified are dead…

DEFENSE – Mr. Prosecutor, the defendant does not feel well! He must undergo dangerous eye surgery...

PROSECUTOR – The defendant was admitting certain things…

CRUPI – Yes, Sir... It could be that I ordered the murders of Nunzio Calabrò and Mario Orefice, for which I have not even been indicted… Why couldn't that be? In fact, let me tell you something: they were two bastards, two lurid sons of bitches, who lived by bullying others, stealing, insulting. They cut half the trees in an orchard of mine. I truly wished them dead. So, then, why couldn't I be the one who ordered their murders? But there's no proof...

DEFENSE – (*Loudly*): I ask the Court to suspend the hearing. I need to talk with the defendant.

CRUPI – (*Without looking at him*) Sir, I know what I must do! It's true, I feel sick, but it does not matter... .I just have a screwed-up heart... the prison doctor is a strange fellow, a mixture between a cop and a poet, he is very cruel when he makes a diagnosis though he can make you visualize it well: he says that my eyesight, rather my whole life is like a rock hanging from a rubber band that's becoming ever thinner. . . My Defense attorney, my illustrious colleague and defender, wants me to ask to be transferred to a hospital. What would I do there? Knowing that they're talking about me without my being able to defend myself? To be cured, to remain a feeble old man, ever more blind? No! I have loved life and have tried to honor it... Now it's about to end, but I want to understand clearly what few things will happen to me...

(*He gets up.*)

You have brought me here and lined me up with those men and I want to stay there until the end.

PROSECUTOR – Those men are murderers, Mr. Crupi. You seem to have regard and benevolence toward them.

(*The defendant walks slowly towards the cage, looking at the other defendants.*)

CRUPI – I feel neither benevolence for them, nor fear or disdain; they are human beings, no worse than others....

(*He turns towards the Prosecutor.*)

Mr. Prosecutor, can't you see what is happening outside, I am referring to the organization of our society...? Can't you see the relationship among men? The same things are happening everywhere... On one side there are the lucky ones, the malicious ones, the corrupt and on the other the defenseless, the dumb and the weak...

PROSECUTOR – And what does it mean.... that murderers must be set free?

CRUPI – Not at all, Mr. Prosecutor! I mean that there are two ways of killing a human being. There are those who kill a human being day after day, by denying them work, schools for their children. They rob them of respect, honor, and the pleasure of life, they take away their home, they stop their children from winning job competitions... They make them beg for forgiveness and mercy. They make them vote for a party they don't even know, for candidates they dislike, they make them say yessir and nosir on command and they take away their conscience. They take away even the dignity of being a man, which is worse than being dead... Mr. Prosecutor, debasing a man in such a way is a hundred times worse than killing him!

(*He takes a few more steps toward the cage, looking at the defendants.*)

So why should I feel disgust or fear for these men that you are accusing of murder? If what you say is true, they killed men who were their enemies... They took away their lives, which is something that never belongs to us and which will be lost anyway, but they left them their dignity, the satisfaction of having lived as men until the end....

(*With the tip of his walking stick he brushes the legs of the boy who's sitting on the bench, next to the cage.*)

Ciao, Totoino...

(*He returns to his seat. At the same time the Defense lawyer comes forward, almost to the center of the Courtroom. He points to defendant Crupi.*)

DEFENSE – I don't know if the accused Mr. Crupi will be able to attend all the other sessions in this trial until the sentencing. Nevertheless, it's right that he be here at this time to hear what I will ask Luciano Salemi, the brother of the murdered ex-Mayor: a witness whom the Prosecution brought here solely to shine a light on Mr. Crupi's human and moral figure for the Court. You all heard him and now I ask that he be brought back to the Courtroom.

DEFENSE – The Court must have a clear possibility of evaluating all that has been said. These are important things for justice...

(*He speaks now from the back of the witness who has already sat down, facing the Court.*)

The Prosecution has called this man to tell us who Emanuele Crupi was, and he told us his opinion. Allow me for a moment to ask the question in reverse...

(*He turns to the defendants' bench.*)

Defendant Crupi, what do you think of this man?

(*The defendant rises slowly.*)

CRUPI – From what I know, he is a man of little worth!
DEFENSE – And in your opinion, when is a man worth little?
CRUPI – When you can buy him for little money!

(The witness smiles imperceptibly. Then adjusts his eyeglasses with his index finger.)

DEFENSE – Thank You!

(Defendant Crupi sits down. The Defense takes one more step closer to the back of the witness.)

DEFENSE – Witness Salemi, listen carefully now, and try to answer my questions concisely. You owned a six-room apartment and five acres of land. Is that correct?
SALEMI – Yes!
DEFENSE – You sold the apartment three years ago and last year you sold the land. Is that right?
SALEMI – Yes.
DEFENSE – What was the money used for? How did you spend it?

(The witness is silent.)

Did you pay off some debts? Please, answer!
SALEMI – Yes!
DEFENSE – I ask you to answer more quickly. Do you know how to play the card game "briscola?"
SALEMI – Yes!
DEFENSE – Do you know how to play "scopone"?
SALEMI – Yes!
DEFENSE – Do you know how to play "zecchinetta"?
SALEMI – Yes.
DEFENSE – Are you aware that "zecchinetta" is a risky game?
SALEMI – Yes.
PROSECUTOR – What does all this have to do with this trial?
DEFENSE – Please, Mr. Prosecutor! (*Turning to the witness.*) Do you play the game of "zecchinetta" sometimes?

(The witness does not answer.)

Isn't it true that you were arrested five times for participating in illegal gambling?

(The witness does not answer.)

And do you know how to play Poker?

SALEMI – Yes!

DEFENSE – Dice, Roulette, Baccarat?

SALEMI – Yes.

DEFENSE – And how many hours a day do you devote to card games in the clubs and bars? Can you describe how you spend your day?

(*The witness does not answer.*)

I'll tell you then! You teach four hours a day, in the morning, as a substitute teacher in the elementary school, then you sleep for a few hours in the afternoon, and from seven at night to two or three in the morning you devote yourself to card games! You play seven, eight, ten hours a day without stopping. You play with anyone and for any sum; you have borrowed money from at least ten different people and I can name each one of them. You are a law school graduate and a legal prosecutor, but you have no more clients. You were a teacher at the local High School, but you were not renewed; your wife has brought two complaints to the police to stop you from gambling. Two months ago she petitioned the Court to record her interdiction against your attempting to gamble away the last piece of property you own. If I am relating facts that are not correct, do tell me!

(*The witness remains silent and unmoving.*)

Professor Salemi, you came here to tell a story of wrongs and you spoke like a man who had seen his noble sentiments trampled by society.... But, what are you, really? A good for nothing, a coward... one day you lost three hundred thousand lire in a Poker game and you started crying before fifty people. Is it true? I asked you if it's true! You must answer loudly if it's true: yes or no?

SALEMI – Yes!

DEFENSE – Mr. Prosecutor, in this trial where the only proofs are the testimonies of a mental deficient and a madman, we rely on moral considerations of a man like him, a failure....

PROSECUTOR – Moral considerations are made by justice!

DEFENSE – That's right, that's right! So let's hear what other moral considerations can be drawn from this witness brought here by the Prosecution. He would have starved to death if he hadn't obtained that substitute teacher position at the elementary school... but do you know how he obtained that job, with whose recommendation? Do you know who pays his salary? The men who are supposed to have killed his brother, the Mayor. He did not say it loud and clear, mind you, but he wanted everyone to know that he meant them. He implored them, of course. In his heart he hates them, but he implored them... He wants to see them dead and buried, but meanwhile he asks for the honor of being their friend, to play cards with them, to have the job of a failure, to be able to sit at the cafe together. Would you please show the photograph?

(A photo is projected against the back of the room, showing a table in an outdoor café and a group of people enjoying themselves. Prof. Salemi is seated among them. There are also some children in the picture.)

There he is! Please note the look of good cheer on his face, how protected he feels in their company.... That man standing on the right, the one with the dark jacket is Luciano Verzì, accused in this room for committing eight murders... and that other man on whose shoulder Professor Salemi is resting his hand, is Carmelo Licitra, the man who was killed with two shots to the head, the father of the boy you brought here to testify.... Even the boy is present in the snapshot...

(To the boy.)

Toti, come forward! Do you recognize that man in the picture... is it your father?

TOTI – Yes, Sir!

DEFENSE – And do you know this man?

TOTI – Yes!

DEFENSE – Was he a friend of your father's?

TOTI – Yes, sir!

DEFENSE – How do you know he was a friend?

TOTI – They took walks together, they played cards together!

DEFENSE – If this man was a friend of your father's, you certainly would know what everybody called him.

TOTI – Yes, Sir. They called him the "King of Clubs"

DEFENSE – The "King of Clubs"! Now, to make absolutely clear how ridiculous are some of the witnesses on whom the Prosecution has relied, I would like to relate how the pretrial judge characterized our witness: "Luciano Salemi, attorney, public relations expert, literary author, teacher." It may seem that the judge is talking about somebody else, but, in fact, he is talking about him. And it's on this Luciano Salemi that the Prosecutor has based his preliminary investigation on the environment, the corruption, the violence, the political fierceness in which the crimes were spawned.... Of course, Luciano Salemi has never stolen anything or killed anyone…there is no evidence nor accusations against him… but this is the type of man he is.

(Returning slowly to his table, he turns to the boy.)

Salvatore Licitra, you may go now…

(*The boy takes leave somewhat awkwardly, then he greets Prof. Salemi.*)

SALEMI – Ciao, Totoino!

(*As the boy is leaving.*)

PROSECUTOR – Prof. Salemi, was this boy a pupil of yours in the first elementary classes?

SALEMI – Yes, Sir. All the boys in the picture were my students. They were all the same age as my son… they played together…

PROSECUTOR – Are you separated from your wife?

SALEMI – Yes, Sir.

PROSECUTOR – Who has custody of your child?

SALEMI – My son is dead, Mr. Prosecutor. He died of typhoid fever a few years ago when he was seven years old.

PROSECUTOR – I am sorry.

SALEMI – Not because he was my child, but he was a most handsome boy… he was also my pupil in school. But that is not the reason why I am attached to those children. Perhaps the gentlemen of the Court don't know it, but the children of my hometown are worth their weight in gold…

DEFENSE – (*Interrupting him*) We know that you wrote a book of poems dedicated to the children of your town... You sold only sixteen copies…! But in this room we are conducting a trial, we are not a literary academy. We can talk only about precise facts…

(*The witness looks at the Court without a word.*)

PROSECUTOR – Prof. Salemi, do you think you have anything to add that has a bearing on the trial?

SALEMI – You are judging events that happened in my hometown… (*he hesitates.*) I would like to make you understand… It's important…

(*He flashes a humble smile as he continues, without moving, to look at the Court.*)

You cannot know what life is in my town. There is nothing there. Nothing ever happens there! There is no industry to hire the unemployed, the soil is barren and abandoned now; there is no water to bathe with and sometimes even to drink. You have never been there, therefore, you can't understand…the squalor….the dead souls….Our statistics are horrendous. In my town we have the highest infant mortality in the country. Many children die of tuberculosis, typhus, or have stunted growth. Their eyes are infected with trachoma.

(*While the witness is talking, the images of the children in the picture on the back wall slowly become larger until their beautiful and sad faces occupy the foreground.*)

A fantastic thing happens though: in my town, in fact, on average more children are born than in any other town in Europe. My town has babies galore. Every month a hundred people die and four hundred new ones are born… Many of them die in infancy but many others survive and continue to grow. Thirty percent remain illiterate and seventy percent become laborers or building helpers… But as soon as these children grow into men there is no more room for them and then they must emigrate. We export them to Paris, Milan, Hamburg. They are extraordinary men capable of working ten, twelve hours a day for little pay and in any climate…

Their labor creates billions… that is what I wanted to say before… Each one of them sends home every month fifty or sixty dollars and the town lives with that money. The people pay the storekeepers, the doctors, the bricklayers who in turn pay their creditors. In the last few yeas we have exported more than ten thousand human beings. In town we kept only the old, the sick, and the elementary school teachers…

You want to know what my town is like? We have a town theater but it is not open; we have a splendid library, but it's in ruin…Who is going to read those books? We have two cinemas three billiards halls, ten cafes…

(*The Defense Attorney interrupts loudly.*)

DEFENSE – Mr. Prosecutor, this is literature!

PROSECUTOR – These are facts, Sir!

DEFENSE – (*Reacting*) These are not the facts that we are interested in!

PROSECUTOR – (*Raising his voice*) Dozens of people were murdered in the midst of these facts.

(*Silence. The witness looks at the Court then resumes.*)

SALEMI – We have nothing, not even water! The water main of the aqueduct caved in underneath the houses. We have been waiting thirty years for them to build a new aqueduct… We get water one hour per week. It is sold in the streets in barrels. The donkey cart with the barrel comes along and dispenses the water: thirty or fifty cents a carafe depending on its size.

There are no sewers to carry away our excrements... Nevertheless people must get rid of their excrements in some ways and so in the middle of any street, small or large, they have dug a channel graded toward the lower part of town so that when they dump the liquid refuse it can flow downward. At dawn or in the middle of the night, every family comes out in silence and dumps their excrements inside the ditch that carries them away from one street to the next…

We have nothing! We have no water in our houses, nor sewers to free ourselves of our own miseries, nor streets to walk on, nor hospitals to take care of the sick…and we don't even have respect for ourselves, no solidarity…that collective strength that desperation sometimes succeeds in creating in peoples' souls. We are dead…

(*The defense interrupts him again.*)

DEFENSE – And did your brother work to bring you back to life?

SALEMI – (*Continuing with the same tone of sadness.*) The truth is that men…

DEFENSE – (*Interrupting him again.*) And did your brother fight to redeem you, to regain your destiny for you?

SALEMI – (*With the same unchanging sadness.*) The truth is that the strongest men, those who could have fought or hold out hope, went away… We exported them so they could send back fifty dollars a month, so we could survive. You know when I see the town swarming with children I'm happy because I think that my town seems wealthy like that...That's why I love them…

You cannot know, you have never seen the children of my town, you've never spoken with them… They are thin, so small and frail. Nevertheless, they will grow and become men. In ten years they will go to Canada or to Australia or to the Belgian mines … There! This is what I wanted to make you understand…

(*He remains silent for a moment. He makes a vague, hesitant gesture while still looking at the Court.*)

Certainly, your Honor, if you go to Germany or to Holland, you will never find so many men with stunted growth or so many dwarfs and deformed men, or murderers. The good health of individuals depends on the food they eat when they are young, and their morals and intelligence as well…did you know that? It's not true that misery and want refine the mind: they simply make it famished, ready to pounce like a wolf, but that is not intelligence, it's a savage instinct. Not even the poetry of the poor means intelligence, it's only a desperation of the soul… the genius of the hungry is useless, cruel, blinded by a thousand problems to survive. We manage only to fight amongst ourselves. That's where our genius triumphs…we fight for everything, for the boundaries of our fields, for a janitor's job, for a deputy's friendship, for being registered in the poor people list, for all the miserable things that for us have an enormous value…and we fight with so much cunning, patience and fierceness that we succeed in defeating one another fatally.

Once in a while, among those who have remained there is someone who rebels and tries to start everything from scratch…

Because you were born in a given place in the world and you are nothing...but you are a human being and you have a right to all the dignity of a man; what you can accomplish remains to be seen...

—My brother was like that. He wanted to change the town...you can't imagine how courageous and hopeful he was. For this reason he rebelled against this life, but he was murdered!

(He slowly removes his eyeglasses.)

—I, on the other hand, am still alive...I am incapable of doing anything, neither to become a murderer, nor to fight against them...

(Silence.)

PROSECUTOR – You may go!

(The witness rises, adjusts his eyeglasses slightly. He bows faintly to the Court. The harsh voice of the Defense stops him before he has a chance to move.)

DEFENSE – Salemi, do you want to tell the Court if your brother, the Mayor, played cards as well?

(The witness remains immobile.)

Answer me! Isn't it true that he too played Poker and zecchinetta in gambling halls, and that he was even more addicted than you? That he even wounded a man in a melee; mortgaged his only house and even went to play in gambling rooms in Palermo?

SALEMI – He was free to do what he wanted!

(The witness again removes his eyeglasses. His eyelids are quivering while the Defense lawyer attacks.)

DEFENSE – And isn't it true that there was a woman in town married to a poor emigrant who had given birth to your brother's child and that your brother was twice accused of flagrant adultery and that once before they attempted to shoot him?

SALEMI – No one ever found out who shot at him...

(The witness remains immobile.)

DEFENSE – Come on, turn around and defend this brother of yours! Look me in the eyes and answer me! Isn't it true that in this town there were at least a hundred people who either because of debts, insults, betrayals, and acts of violence could have had an interest in killing him?

SALEMI – They killed him because he fought back (*breathlessly*)… They killed him because he fought back…

DEFENSE – Salemi, you who are devoured by pity and love for poor people, why don't you tell the Court about that petition signed by two thousand citizens asking the Courts to remove your brother?… Isn't it true that that petition contained your signature as well? Prof. Luciano Salemi, Esquire…They wanted him impeached because he was a violent and corrupt man, a cheat …that's what the petition said… and it had your signature too! Come forward, Salemi, and tell the Court how on the day of your brother's funeral your mother spit in your face before everyone…

SALEMI – My mother is already dead…

DEFENSE – Your mother wanted you to kill those who had killed your brother. That's what she was screaming before everyone…

SALEMI – I could not do that…What did I have to do with that whole matter?

PROSECUTOR – They had killed your brother!

DEFENSE – Your mother spit in your face for this reason!

(*The witness opens his mouth as if to say something, but remains silent.*)

DEFENSE – (*Relentlessly*) Why didn't you go before the judges to tell them the murderers' names? Go on, Salemi, tell us those names now.

SALEMI – (*Interrupting him with a scream.*) My brother…

DEFENSE – (*Interrupting him in turn.*) Go on, speak!

SALEMI – (*Screaming*) I burned that dossier of his…I don't know anything… I burned it!

DEFENSE – Continue!

SALEMI – (*Screaming blindly.*) My brother rebelled and they killed him…you named a lousy little street after him… He was a real man, but you, what are you?

(*He gasps for air, for the words he wants to speak.*)

I burned that dossier… without ever reading it.

(*With desperation, facing the Court.*)

Now you're holding me here, all against me and you're destroying me… but I'm like you…if you see a man killed, you shutter your windows so you don't see who did it.

(*He senses the Carabiniere approaching from behind and moves aside with a shudder screaming.*)

—I'm like you! A miserable, cowardly, little man…

(When he feels the Carabiniere's hand touching him on his shoulder he twists like a serpent but his feet remains immobile. He remains frozen while letting out a heart-rending scream. Suddenly he stops, he starts out as if to flee, but he goes toward the defendants' cage and he stops there emitting another horrible scream of fear. He turns around and exits.

In the last five minutes the light has been lowered imperceptibly until the room is bathed in only a yellowish halo. In the shadows only the picture of those beautiful children's faces remains lit. The curtain falls.)

Act III

(Shouting that is growing in intensity is heard even with the curtain down. It is a loud, continuous, violent, and collective shout that involves all the defendants. The courtroom is dark. The corners are almost totally in the dark. Down at the end, seated on a bench, the mother of Venero Alicata. In the foreground, a youthful man with long black hair and a dark complexion is seated facing the Jury.)

PROSECUTOR– *(Pounding the table twice)* Silence!

(The shouting continues for a moment, then, dies out almost suddenly. The defense attorney approaches from the back wall toward the back of the defendant.)

DEFENSE – Gentlemen of the Jury, this is Rosario Vacirca, the main witness for the Prosecution. Don't miss a word of what he will say because this whole trial, this bloody pyramid of living and dead people, rests on him. At the end, I will demonstrate to you that he is insane.

(Remains in darkness next to his table.)

PROSECUTOR– Rosario Vacirca, son of the late Dominic, 28 years of age?

VACIRCA – Yes, Sir.

PROSECUTOR– You are accused of voluntary manslaughter, premeditated and aggravated murder, complicity in another aggravated murder and attempted murder, possession of firearms, resistance and violence against a public official, and criminal association. Are you aware of the charges?

VACIRCA – Yes, Sir.

PROSECUTOR– I don't know what your answers will be now before the Jury, but I ask you if you clearly understand the importance of your testimony…

(The defendant remains silent. The defendants in the cage start a whispering that grows in intensity.)

PROSECUTOR– Silence!

(The mumbling dies down and the Prosecutor continues.)

The transcripts describe your capture as follows: "Rosario Vacirca, who had a warrant out for his arrest, fired his gun several times against the police who had ordered him to halt, fatally wounding Officer Giovanni Busà. The bloody confrontation ended when the police finally subdued Vacirca who put up fierce resistance even though he had been hit in the leg with three bullets." This transcript was written a few hours after your capture. Have you anything to add or any objection?

VACIRCA – No, Sir.

PROSECUTOR– The Prosecution states that on November 18, at 9:00 PM, you fired two shots from a sawed-off shotgun at the head of convicted felon Carmelo Licitra. Do you confirm your confession?

(The mumbling that had begun out of the crowd in the cage suddenly grows in intensity before the defendant is able to answer.)

Silence! Or I will have you removed from the Courtroom!

VACIRCA – Yes, Sir, I confirm my confession.

PROSECUTOR– The prosecution finally states that on a March evening of last year, acting together with felon Luciano Verzì, who physically carried out the crime, you took part in the murder of Chief Inspector Ettore Florena, shot with five bullets. Do you now confirm this confession, as well?

(As the Prosecutor began stating this last charge, an ominous rumbling is heard from the cage that grows so loud that his last words are almost drowned out and culminates with a terrible howl when the defendant opens his mouth to answer. The defendant remains motionless staring before him. The Prosecutor stands up.)

Out, out, clear the room!

(All the defendants are standing. At first slowly, then hurriedly, continuously directing their shouting against the defendant they leave the room. The thud of a heavy door closing is heard. Absolute silence. The defendant has remained unmoving.)

PROSECUTOR– Do you confirm your confession?

VACIRCA – Yes, Sir, I do!

PROSECUTOR– *(Slowly)* Rosario Vacirca, we will now reconstruct the facts, one by one. Listen very carefully to the questions and answer them clearly.

(The defendant is silent.)

Do you know Giovanni Savoca?

VACIRCA – Yes, Sir.

PROSECUTOR– Who was he?

VACIRCA – He was a cattle and land broker. He was an old man, at least seventy years old.

PROSECUTOR– What else do you know about him?

VACIRCA – He was well-known in town…He had asked me to do some work in his fields. He was well off…

PROSECUTOR– What else?

VACIRCA – He was mixed up in politics. He liked to boss people around... He had been elected town Councilman...

PROSECUTOR– What dealings did you have with him?

VACIRCA – I already said it. I did some bricklayering work for him in his fields. We played cards a few times. That's all!...One evening I was sitting at a table in the café and he came to sit next to me...

PROSECUTOR– You must relate this episode with extreme care. Try to recall his exact words...

VACIRCA – I was alone at the table and Giovanni Savoca came to sit next to me. He started saying: "You're not working... you don't even have enough money to emigrate, but I consider you a friend. Listen to me carefully: 'Have you got it in you to kill Carmelo Licitra?'"

PROSECUTOR– Did he just come out with this? Didn't he talk about other things too?

VACIRCA – No, Sir. He said just like that, measuring his words. "Everything's ready," he said. "I'll even give you the sawed-off shotgun."

PROSECUTOR– What did you answer him?

VACIRCA – Nothing! I said nothing. I had a cup of coffee before me and I continued sipping it slowly...

PROSECUTOR– What did Giovanni Savoca tell you then? I want to know his exact words...

VACIRCA – Giovanni Savoca added: "Here is five hundred thousand lire, counted out. I'll tell you the exact night. While we're playing cards, you'll go out for 15 minutes, hide behind the church doorway, and as Carmelo Licitra passes by, you blow his head off, then you come back to play cards. I'll testify you were with me the whole time. Who can accuse you of anything? You don't even know him, you've never spoken to him..."

PROSECUTOR– Go on! What happened then?

(The defendant pauses for a moment, as though he were trying to remember the exact words.)

VACIRCA – I asked him: "Why should I kill Carmelo Licitra? What did he do?" Giovanni Savoca answered me: "That's none of your business, because if you know why, it's as if you had a motive for killing him. He is a dishonest man, an ass-kissing clown. What...? Are you afraid? If that's the case, I'll take off...but you know how these things are: the chances to know your true friends are few in life..."

PROSECUTOR– So then, did you accept?

VACIRCA – I was afraid. Killing Carmelo Licitra didn't bother me, but

I was afraid and Giovanni Savoca told me then: "What are you afraid of? You didn't even know Carmelo Licitra, not even to say 'Good morning or good night'. The sawed off shotgun wasn't even yours. There must be at least 200 guys in town who could have killed him. So what are they going to do? Arrest us all?"

DEFENSE – (*Suddenly.*) Rosario Vacirca, you really didn't know Carmelo Licitra?

VACIRCA – No, Sir. I had never spoken to him. I knew who he was, but that's all. I saw him during elections. I saw him a few times in the café or at the union hall.

DEFENSE – You never had any occasion to speak with him?

VACIRCA – No, Sir. Not a single word! What could we have said to each other?

DEFENSE – You didn't know him, you never exchanged a single word with him, he never insulted you, never treated you badly or hurt you in any way. Is that right?

VACIRCA – Yes, Sir.

DEFENSE – Did you know he was married and that he was the father of two children?

VACIRCA – Yes, Sir.

DEFENSE – Yet, you murdered him! You shot him from two yards away with a sawed-off shotgun loaded with pellets. You blew his head off... Is that right?

(*The defendant remains silent.*)

I'm asking you if you are confirming your confession...

VACIRCA – Yes, Sir.

DEFENSE – Another question. You didn't know the real motive for the killing. For whom did you kill Carmelo Licitra? Did you try to find out ?

VACIRCA – I asked Giovanni Savoca and he answered that I was doing it for him. It was something that mattered to him.

DEFENSE – But did you think it was true?

(*The defendant remains silent.*)

Answer me. Did you think it was the truth?

VACIRCA –No, Sir. I imagined there were other interests behind it.

DEFENSE – Whose interests? Continue!

VACIRCA – I figured Emanuele Crupi's interests.

DEFENSE – And why Mr. Crupi?

VACIRCA – Because Giovanni Savoca was a loyal crony of his. He had worked with him for thirty years as a broker, a field caretaker…

DEFENSE – And, in your opinion, what motive would Mr. Crupi have to have Carmelo Licitra killed?

VACIRCA – I said I didn't know. Savoca didn't tell me and I never asked him again.

DEFENSE – I ask that defendants Crupi and Verzì be brought back into the Courtroom for cross-examination.

(The Prosecutor nods in agreement and down at the end a door is opened. Defendant Verzì appears a bit hesitantly, looking around to understand what is happening. He then proceeds to sit down on the lower bench. Behind him, moving more slowly, appears Emanuele Crupi who proceeds to sit at the center of the upper bench, almost in the shadows.)

PROSECUTOR– Go on, Vacirca. Continue!

DEFENSE – Giovanni Savoca paid you half a million lire and you killed Carmelo Licitra…Was it an easy hit, was it quick?

(The defendant does not answer.)

I asked you if it was an easy and quick thing…

VACIRCA – I did what they told me to do. I knew they had left the shotgun behind a wall in the orchard… I found it and hid behind the doorway. When Carmelo Licitra passed by, I fired the two barrels in the direction of his head.

DEFENSE – And then?

VACIRCA – Then, nothing. I did not wait to see if I had hit him or if he was dead. I started running and threw the shotgun behind the orchard's wall, as they told me. I returned to the cafe from the bathroom door and I resumed playing cards with Giovanni Savoca.

DEFENSE – The whole night?

VACIRCA – The whole night. Half an hour later, an acquaintance came in and said that someone had killed Carmelo Licitra. Giovanni Savoca then put the deck of cards on the table and with a mournful look said: "Really? I wonder what in hell he did to get killed!" And we resumed playing cards.

DEFENSE – And what happened in the days that followed?

VACIRCA – Nothing. The police arrested six or seven people, but after two months the District Attorney released them. Nothing happened until one night Giovanni Savoca was killed. They shot him from a car while he was returning home on his bike.

DEFENSE – When you learned of Giovanni Savoca's death, what did you feel? Sorrow for the death of a friend or fear?

VACIRCA – Sorrow? No! Savoca was not a friend to me. He was an old man. He had played his part in life by then.

DEFENSE – Did you feel fear then?

VACIRCA – Fear of what? I thought, instead, that Savoca was the only man who knew I had killed Licitra and now he was dead. He could not talk any more...

DEFENSE – So, you felt a sense of satisfaction?

VACIRCA – I didn't say that.

DEFENSE – What did you mean, then?

VACIRCA –I felt more secure. Any man in my shoes would have felt more secure.

DEFENSE – (*To the Jury*) Pay attention! This is the kind of man he is. He is saying he murdered a man he didn't even know to earn enough to live on for four or five months—enough to play cards and go with a whore once in a while— He blasted Licitra's head off, and the death of the man who had put him up to it does not cheer him up! No…let it not be said that he would have such base feelings! Instead, he gets a sense of security from it…This he freely admits… a sense of reassurance. He feels impregnable as though he were inside a steel barrel. So what happened at this point?

(*The defendant does not reply.*)

I asked you what happened at this point? Or don't you remember your statement any more? Do I have to read it from the transcripts?

VACIRCA – One night I met Luciano Verzì …

DEFENSE – (*To the Jury*) Pay attention! At this point, a fantastic event takes place: the defendant meets Luciano Verzì! The whole trial, put together with great effort with hundreds of facts and characters, facts glued with a strand of saliva…names, motives, murders… a huge pyramid of living and dead people, rests on the fantastic tale you are about to hear…

(*To the defendant.*)

So, one night you met Luciano Verzì…

VACIRCA – Yes, Sir.. I met him on a bus to Palermo. There were only five passengers: three women, up front near the ticket controller, and the two of us at the back …

(*Defendant Verzì shouts in a loud voice.*)

VERZÌ – It's a lie, it's a lie! I don't know him. I have never spoken to him. He is a poor slob. Where are the witnesses?

PROSECUTOR– Keep quiet, Verzì!

DEFENSE – Was Luciano Verzì a friend of yours?

VACIRCA – No.

DEFENSE – And what was your opinion of him?

VACIRCA – A hoodlum! I knew he had worked for some time in the naval shipyards in Palermo, then he returned to town where they had given him a job as an assistant in the agricultural agency, but he was a hoodlum... everybody knew it...

PROSECUTOR – Continue!

VACIRCA – Luciano Verzì suddenly told me: "I know you killed Carmelo Licitra! Giovanni Savoca paid you half a million lire, but Savoca is dead now...You have no one to look out for you any more."

DEFENSE – Then, what?

VACIRCA – Luciano Verzì added: "Do you know why they had you kill Carmelo Licitra?" When I didn't answer, he added: "He'd been involved in the murder of Venero Alicata, and was becoming cocky. That's why they had him killed."

DEFENSE – Are those his exact words?

VACIRCA – That's what he said, exactly! Then he added: "There's something else you don't know: I'm the one who shot Alicata!"

(Rosalia Alicata from her bench lets out a scream, directed against Luciano Verzì.)

ROSALIA – It was you who killed him, degenerate beast, and you don't have the courage to admit it. At least you could have boasted you killed Venero Alicata!...

PROSECUTOR– Rosalia Alicata, I order you to keep quiet!

ROSALIA – Mr. Prosecutor, he is the murderer! They gave him money and he killed my son. How is it that you still don't believe it?

PROSECUTOR– Be quiet or I will have you removed from the Courtroom.

ROSALIA – How could you send away Venero Alicata's mother? With what conscience?

(She stops talking and sits down again on her bench. Throughout this exchange, Verzì and Vacirca remained silent and immobile.)

PROSECUTOR– Rosario Vacirca, continue!

VACIRCA – Luciano Verzì told me: "I'm the one who shot Alicata! I also knew too many things and sooner or later Giovanni Savoca would have had me killed. I killed him before he could think about killing me."

VERZÌ – *(Suddenly shouting.)* It's not true! It's a lie!

(He comes forward with his hair ruffled. The Carabinieri hold him back, as he

struggles to approach closer to the Jury. Meanwhile he screams.)

It's not true! It's not true! You must let me talk...I didn't even know Venero Alicata...Can't you see it's a lie?

PROSECUTOR– Take him back to his seat!

(*The defendant resists passively, sticks his head forward toward the Jury.*)

VERZÌ – Why are you holding me back? I'm not hurting anyone, but I must be allowed to defend myself. Your Honor, I have been tortured for two years...I can't take it any more! Don't listen to that bastard!

PROSECUTOR – Put handcuffs on him!

(*Reacting with fear, Verzì frees himself from the Carabinieri and retreats.*)

VERZÌ – No, no, your Honor. Please, forgive me, I'll return to my seat and keep quiet.

(*He resumes his place on the bench.*)

PROSECUTOR– (*To defendant Vacirca.*) Verzì confessed to you that he was Venero Alicata's killer...

VACIRCA – That's what he said.

DEFENSE – And you said nothing even after this revelation?

VACIRCA – Nothing! I thought it was funny business, not on the level, but it could also have been true. The only thing I did not understand was why he volunteered this information. In fact, at the end he told me: "You know? I was supposed to kill you, too." Terrific, I thought, but meanwhile I was thinking: the minute he makes a wrong move I'll shoot him right between the eyes.

DEFENSE – What happened instead?

VACIRCA – Instead, Luciano Verzì started laughing. "Don't worry!" He said. "I know you're a good man and I'm going to give you the chance to prove what you can do. I need you to come along with me one night, that's all. I have to keep an eye on someone, see what he does and who he meets and I need you to watch my back. But if someone follows me you must shoot him."

DEFENSE – Who was the man he had to spy on?

VACIRCA – He didn't tell me that night.

DEFENSE – But did he promise? Did he ever give you any money?

VACIRCA – No, never.

DEFENSE – So, he didn't tell you what he was supposed to do, nor did he ever promise or give you any money, and you still accepted to go with him?

VACIRCA – I had realized one thing: in the midst of all that was happening I was alone.

DEFENSE – What do you mean, alone?

VACIRCA – Alone…without anyone to watch out for me…they could have torn me to pieces any time they wanted…

DEFENSE – So you accepted to follow Verzì. When did it happen?

VACIRCA – The evening of March 14.

DEFENSE – Was it March 14 or 15?

VACIRCA – 14 or 15, I don't remember any more…

DEFENSE – What day of the week was it?

VACIRCA – It must have been a Saturday.

DEFENSE – No, it could have not been either the 14 or the 15, because those days were Wednesday and Thursday respectively. What time of the day was it?

VACIRCA – It must have been nine PM. It was dark out.

DEFENSE – But it was already dark at seven PM…

VACIRCA – I don't remember any more…

DEFENSE – Was it raining that night?

(The defendant does not reply.)

I asked you if it was raining.

VACIRCA – I don't know!

DEFENSE – How can you not know? How is it possible? A man who stays out all day would remember if it was raining!

VACIRCA – Maybe it was raining. I don't know…

DEFENSE – And when did you realize that Luciano Verzì was not there to spy on a man, but to kill him?

VACIRCA – When he fired the first shot against him!

DEFENSE – How many shots did he fire?

VACIRCA – I think three or four, one after the other…

(Luciano Verzì shouts from the cage.)

VERZÌ – Why are you telling these lies? You fucking, goddamned bastard…The night of the killing I was at a funeral. I got the proof…

(He does not dare to stand up, though.)

PROSECUTOR – Go on, Vacirca, tell us exactly what happened!

VACIRCA – We got to the city boulevard and hid the motorcycle beyond the curve …

VERZÌ – It's not true! You fucking bastard!

(With a faltering shout he hurls himself against the defendant, but the Carabinieri grab him by his jacket from behind, lifting him practically in the air. Verzì quickly becomes

inert, but he continues to struggle with his head. He shouts in anguish.)

I'll crush your head! You have to repeat it before me! I'll take your life, you miserable bastard!

PROSECUTOR– (*shouting*) Put handcuffs on him!

(*Verzì nearly bends backward and lets out a shriek of fear.*)

VERZÌ – Let me go! Your Honor, tell them to let me go! I'm going to sit down on the bench and I'll be quiet. You can say anything you want…

(*Struggling with his head, and lifting his arms high in the air, Verzì tries to avoid being handcuffed by the Carabinieri, but he feels the cuffs' click. He looks like he wants to tear them off with his teeth. He vomits.*)

VERZÌ – I'm choking, help…take off these handcuffs!

(*He lifts his handcuffed arms high in the air as the Carabinieri drag him to his bench. He is breathing with great difficulty.*)

Help! I am sick! You're cutting my wrists…I'm bleeding!

(*He slumps on the bench and remains motionless. Only his very low, continuous moan is heard. Silence. Rosario Vacirca in all this time has continued to look toward the Jury without moving or saying a word.*)

PROSECUTOR– So you arrived then at the city boulevard and you hid the motorcycle beyond the curve. Go on, Vacirca…

VACIRCA – There was no one in the boulevard. We stayed hidden behind the trees until we saw a man and a woman approaching on the opposite sidewalk. At that time, Verzì told me: "You stay hidden behind here, but be careful!" and he ran across the street, hiding on the other side…In the dark I could not see him any more. Suddenly, as soon as the couple reached my height I saw the flash of a gun and the man fell to his knees as if he had tripped. The woman also fell after him. There were two or three more gun flashes and I realized that the man was already dead. I thought the woman was dead too. I did not understand from which side Verzì had run away and I crossed the street, but at that moment the woman got on her knees next to the body and called me.

DEFENSE –What do you mean, "called" you?

VACIRCA – She repeated the word "help" twice.

DEFENSE – How far were you from her?

VACIRCA – Ten, twelve yards…

DEFENSE – Did you see her face well?

VACIRCA – It was dark. There was only a street lamp, but I was able to make out her features…

DEFENSE – Did you move closer?

VACIRCA – No. I continued to run and I jumped the wall behind the row of trees. I immediately saw Luciano Verzì and we started running through the fields until we reached the curve in the road where we had hidden the motorcycle…

PROSECUTOR– What happened then?

VACIRCA – We reached the point where the boulevard crosses the national road where there was a FIAT 1100 parked near the water trough with its headlights off. "I am taking the motorcycle," said Luciano Verzì. "You get in the car. It will take you to the center of town. This way we won't be seen together." Inside the car there was a man, but I could not see him at first because of the darkness. Luciano Verzì opened the door and just said to him: "This is my friend. Take him to the center of town, then you can leave."

PROSECUTOR– Nothing else?

VACIRCA – No, Sir. Nothing else. He went away on his motorcycle without putting the headlight on and we left in the car.

PROSECUTOR– Did you know the man driving the car?

VACIRCA – No, Sir. I had never seen him before.

PROSECUTOR– And what did he say to you?

VACIRCA – Nothing! He kept driving without a word. Finally I began to make out his face in the dark. He was a thin man with a little moustache, once in a while he whistled a little tune, he seemed in a good mood, but he never said a word. Only at one point he asked me for a cigarette and said: "So what did you do tonight with Luciano Verzì?" "Nothing," I answered. "We took care of a couple of business deals!" "What kind of deals? Women?" he asked and started laughing in a weird way. That's all. After that he said nothing more…

DEFENSE – How long did the ride take?

VACIRCA – Half an hour, three quarters of an hour…

DEFENSE – And in all that time he said nothing else?

VACIRCA – Nothing.

DEFENSE – Is it possible that you did not ask him anything either?

VACIRCA – What interest would I have in that? In fact, I was trying to bury my head in my overcoat so he could not see my face. When we got to town, he stopped in a deserted street and I got off: "Good night!" "Good night!"

PROSECUTOR– And did you ever learn who that man was?

VACIRCA – Yes, Sir. I know now. It was Filippo Giacalone!

DEFENSE – (*Protesting quickly in a loud voice.*) This is not in the transcripts! It can't be admitted! It's crazy!

(*The voices are heard almost simultaneously.*)

PROSECUTOR– It's another piece of evidence!
VACIRCA – I recognized him only during the past few weeks.
DEFENSE – It's a cowardly act! Another lie!
PROSECUTOR– It's a confession heard in the courtroom, a decisive confession…

(*The Defense Attorney laughs out of anger and disdain. And with his hands draws a circle in the air.*)

DEFENSE – Ahhhh! Not bad! It's a well-rehearsed madness!
PROSECUTOR– And when did you realize that the driver was Giacalone?
VACIRCA – The first day of the trial, in the security cell in the basement. I recognized him right away and I told him: "You're the one who drove me in the car." He kept denying it, but I was sure. "You gave me a lift the night they killed the Inspector and you were in it with Luciano Verzì. You spoke to him in front of me." He continued to deny it, but I had recognized him, I was certain of it. He was even wearing the same ring on his finger. Everything matched.
DEFENSE – (*With sarcasm.*) Of course… He was certain of it. That night he had even managed to see the ring on his finger. Everything matched…Everything except the fact that Giacalone has always denied it…
VACIRCA – I spoke to him only once…
DEFENSE – You're a liar, Vacirca! A coward!
VACIRCA – Bring him here before me! He has to deny it here in front of me, if he has the courage. I'm going to provide more evidence, I'll tell him how he was dressed!
DEFENSE – Are you finished, Vacirca? Do you have any more crazy things to invent?

(*Hearing the voice of the prosecutor, Vacirca turns around.*)

PROSECUTOR– And did you know who the murdered man was?

(*Vacirca opens and closes his eyes. He did not understand the question. The Prosecutor insists.*)

PROSECUTOR– Before meeting Giacalone, did Verzì tell you the name of the man he had killed?

VACIRCA – (*Breathlessly*) No. While we were running away, I asked him. I wanted to know. "Shut up! Shut up!" He kept saying.

DEFENSE – So then you only found out the next morning that the murdered man was Inspector Florena?

VACIRCA – Yes, Sir. I saw also the pictures in the papers and I recognized his wife, the woman who was with him.

PROSECUTOR– And even afterwards Luciano Verzì did not tell why he had killed the Inspector?

VACIRCA – No, never. I was certain that he did not even know himself. They had told him to kill him and he did.

VERZÌ – (*Interrupting him*) It's not true!

(Vacirca jumps to his feet. He almost falls because he is limping.)

VACIRCA – (*Drowning him out with his shout*) And, I say it's true. It is true!

PROSECUTOR– (*Over his shout*) So then he told you who had ordered the killing… Come on...his name!

VACIRCA – (*Breathlessly*) Emanuele Crupi, the lawyer. That's what he said to me! This too could have been another lie, a buffoon's joke… but that is what he told me!

(*Vacirca has remained standing next to the chair. He falters a bit because of the effort required to stand on a lame leg. The questions and answers now proceed swiftly, unceasingly.*)

DEFENSE – Do you know Mr. Crupi?

VACIRCA – Yes, Sir. I worked for him as a bricklayer.

DEFENSE – And did he pay you on time?

VACIRCA – Yes, he paid me…

DEFENSE – Did he ever threaten you, insult you, beat you, made fun of you?

VACIRCA – No, never.

DEFENSE – Did he answer your greetings, did he pay you a correct salary, was he courteous, respectful?

VACIRCA – Yes, Sir.

(*He is exhausted by the effort of standing.*)

DEFENSE – Have you ever heard, with your own ears, that he ordered people killed? Did you ever see him kill anyone with his own hands?

VACIRCA – No, Sir.

DEFENSE – But you did see Luciano Verzì kill with his own hands, didn't you?

VACIRCA – Yes, Sir.

VACIRCA – You saw him with your own two eyes, isn't that true?
VACIRCA – Yes.
DEFENSE – He shot four times…one, two, three, four.. didn't he?
VACIRCA – Yes, Sir. Four shots!
DEFENSE – Stop talking now. Don't say another word, Rosario Vacirca!

(*He has advanced a few steps.*)

Mr. Prosecutor, this is the only man who's offered a single valid proof, that is, the only accusation confirmed and reiterated in this trial. So allow me for a moment to assess before the honorable Jury what this man whom you refuse to declare insane has stated so far…

(*He keeps his eyes on the defendant as he is talking. The defendant once in a while falters on his lame leg.*)

First of all he claims that he killed Carmelo Licitra citing only one witness: the man who charged him with the crime, Giovanni Savoca, someone who cannot say either yes or no, a dead man! And you heard the way he related his crime: "I give you half a million lire and you kill Carmelo Licitra…— All right!"

Everything runs like clockwork: He leaves the café, finds the shotgun, the victim passes right before him one yard away, exactly on schedule and Rosario Vacirca shoots him, throws away the shotgun, returns to the café and resumes playing cards…

"You know, someone killed Carmelo Licitra," someone announces. "Is that right? I wonder what he had done!" And they continue to play…The whole thing is insane and yet up to this point it could be true…these are men with a heart of stone. But the story becomes ever more insane. On a bus going to Palermo, Rosario Vacirca meets Luciano Verzì… "I know you killed Carmelo Licitra. Let's see what you're capable of doing now? I have to keep an eye on a man!" The whole dialogue like this between two men who barely know each other… They go and Luciano Verzì, lying in ambush ten yards away, kills Chief Inspector Ettore Florena before Vacirca's eyes… Vacirca cites the dates of the 14 or 15 of March—mind you, he does not recall the day exactly—he maintains that the killing took place at 9:00 PM when in reality it happened at 7:00 PM and finally he is unsure as to how many bullets were fired. He stated three or four and instead there were six shots fired that night. He related the killing exactly as someone who had read about it in the newspaper …

VACIRCA – (*Shouting in the direction of the Jury.*) I saw him with my own eyes!

DEFENSE – (*Continuing in a louder voice.*) He also read that the widow saw a man crossing the street and he claims to be that man. When the widow was asked to identify him, she recognized him! So then, Mr. Prosecutor, let us call this widow who has made hundreds of journalist rave about her. Let us call this fragile and tender woman, who was arrested at first on suspicion of having plotted her husband's murder, imprisoned, and acquitted…Let's see this sorrowful and romantic feminine figure, Mrs. Virna Santalco, Inspector Florena's widow.

PROSECUTOR– Vacirca, stay down there!

(*Rosario Vacirca limps his way close to the defendants' bench as the widow appears from the right.*)

PROSECUTOR– Come forward!

(*The widow approaches slowly, hesitantly. She stops at the center before the Jury. She is dressed in black with a black transparent silk kerchief around her face. She is wearing black glasses.*)

PROSECUTOR – Virna Santalco, wife of the late Inspector Florena, 29 years of age?

WIDOW– Yes.

DEFENSE – Madam, I hope you will excuse me for asking you a few strange and embarrassing questions, but I am sure you too want to learn the truth…

WIDOW– Yes.

DEFENSE – Madam, you no longer reside in the city where your husband was killed, is that right?

WIDOW– Yes, for some time now.

DEFENSE – Why did you move?

WIDOW– I work as a social assistant in a public agency…

DEFENSE – Please excuse me, Madam! Do you remember your husband with the same tenderness as before?

WIDOW– Why shouldn't I? Why are you asking me this question?

DEFENSE – Let me rephrase the question! Are you in love? I mean, are you in love at this time?

PROSECUTOR– What is the meaning of these questions?

DEFENSE – It's odd, Mr. Prosecutor, that you can't guess it. Mrs. Florena, on the other hand, has surely understood it…Oh Mrs. Florena certainly loved her husband with tenderness and to see him stretched out dead at her feet must have been heartbreaking… but life continues beyond the grave…Mrs. Florena might need, in fact, might be in a hurry to show that the murderer has already been identified and that she never saw him... But, Mrs. Florena, you must not be in a hurry here, you can't say a single wrong word...This is why I asked you if you had feelings for a different man...

WIDOW– I do not intend to answer ...You have no right...

DEFENSE – Oh Madam, I know the answer, but this was sufficient for me. If your feelings for your poor husband were still intact, you would not have hesitated in saying so...

PROSECUTOR – Counsel, your questions seem designed to intimidate the witness. I ask the witness to disregard them.

DEFENSE – I too ask the witness to disregard them...

(*Harshly*)

I would be grateful to you, Madam, if you took off the veil and the glasses when you address the Court.

(*Slowly the woman takes off her glasses and the kerchief. A mass of black hair falls on her shoulders. She appears younger, paler and more diaphanous. She appears extremely beautiful, but cold and unmoving.*)

DEFENSE – Madam, do you know attorney Emanuele Crupi personally?

WIDOW – No.

DEFENSE –Do you know if your husband had any connections or business dealings with Emanuele Crupi?

WIDOW – No, never. I never asked my husband anything.

DEFENSE – Did your husband ever speak to you about him?

WIDOW – Never!

DEFENSE – Did he ever speak to you about Luciano Verzì?

WIDOW – No.

DEFENSE – Therefore, you don't know Luciano Verzì. You have never seen him. Is that right?

WIDOW – Yes.

DEFENSE – Did your husband sometimes seem nervous or frightened?

WIDOW – My husband was never afraid...

DEFENSE – Let's say, then, worried on account of his work?

WIDOW – Yes, sometimes, it happened.

DEFENSE – And did he ever tell you why? Was he upset with someone?

WIDOW – He kept saying that his hands were tied, he said that hoodlums dominated even in politics and that wherever he touched he found corrupt and dirty people. He was bitter...

DEFENSE – And did he ever name any of the corrupt people, the hoodlums, the people who tied his hands?

WIDOW – My husband never mentioned any names. I never asked him anything. I could not help him.

DEFENSE – You stated that he was embittered, but that he had no worries or fear. If that is so, why did he ask to be transferred to the capital a month before his murder?

WIDOW – That's what he decided to do.

DEFENSE – No. You must tell us the exact reasons.

WIDOW – They were personal reasons. These are intimate memories... I have the right...

DEFENSE – (*Interrupting her.*) In this room no one has rights. Everything that is connected with the life and death of others no longer belongs to you. Madam, you must explain why your husband asked to be transferred to Rome or I will have to read the transcripts word for word. You know how brutal they were.

WIDOW – My husband was convinced that I no longer loved him.

DEFENSE – Continue!

WIDOW – That I had taken another man as a lover... He wanted to move to another city where no one knew us.

DEFENSE – Mrs. Florena, you did not tell the *Carabinieri* what your husband's anguish was about... You told them instead that your husband wanted a transfer because he felt persecuted by some politicians and criminals... That was false then?

(*The widow does not answer and the Defense insists in a louder voice.*)

Madam, we have men here with their lives on the line... Your husband wanted to move away to avoid facing his shame. You must recognize this, Mrs. Florena!

WIDOW – (*Frightened, protesting.*) He had decided to move even before that happened. That is over now, but you continue to insult me. I don't know now what I told the *Carabinieri*... I don't remember any more!

(*She shakes a bit as she looks at the Jury.*)

DEFENSE – (*Now softly, but without relenting.*) Forgive me, Madam, if the duties of my office cannot allow me to be more compassionate than I would like. But I still must ask you some details that perhaps will be painful... Do you remember the date and exact time of the murder?

WIDOW – March 18 at 7:00 PM.

DEFENSE – You were walking along the poorly lit boulevard, right? You held your husband's arm and there was no one in the street…

WIDOW – Yes.

DEFENSE – Do you recall if your husband was anxious, frightened?

WIDOW – No. He seemed to be in a hurry to get home because he was tired, but he did not seem frightened to me, not even that night…

DEFENSE – But in the outside pocket of his overcoat they found his pistol with a bullet in the chamber and the safety off. Evidently he was holding the gun at the moment of the assault, but he did not have time to use it.

WIDOW – I did not know he was carrying a pistol in his pocket.

DEFENSE – "A man suddenly appeared from behind a tree and began firing against my husband who almost fell on me…I was screaming in terror and that man continued firing until my husband fell to the ground carrying me down with him. I tried to lift him up, but I noticed that his chest was full of blood…" Madam, is this the statement you gave to the District Attorney?

WIDOW – Yes.

DEFENSE – "The murderer had disappeared." Is this also your statement?

WIDOW – Yes.

DEFENSE – "But suddenly I saw another man running across from the other side of the street and I called out to him for help, but he continued running and disappeared in the dark…" Is this correct?

WIDOW – Yes.

DEFENSE – In the District Attorney's office, in full daylight and just two yards away, when you faced the man who had confessed of being the one you saw that tragic night, did you recognize him?

WIDOW – Yes, I recognized him.

DEFENSE – Thank you.

(*The widow remains silent for a moment as though waiting for other questions. Then she bows lightly to the Jury and starts to leave, but the voice of the Defense Attorney stops her and she turns around.*)

DEFENSE – Stop where you are, Madam! One moment, please! Don't take another step forward…. Do you see the cage before you? In it there are three men: one is accused of having had your husband killed, and you have never seen him or spoken to him. Another man is accused of having killed your husband and you cannot identify him because you said you never saw his face! And the third is finally the man who crossed the street as your husband was dying and you saw his face. You already recognized him before the District Attorney. You must tell us now which of the three men he is…

(*The widow looks at them silently and slowly puts on her glasses, but the Defense stops her…*)

DEFENSE – No, Madam, take off those glasses. You did not have glasses the night of the murder.

WIDOW – (*A few seconds of silence. With a tired gesture, the widow indicates Luciano Verzì.*) I think it's him.

DEFENSE – Do you think or are you certain?

WIDOW – I said I think.

DEFENSE – You cannot make a mistake. Look at him carefully!

WIDOW – How can I tell him apart?

DEFENSE – And that night, in the darkness, terror-stricken by all that was happening around you, how did you manage to make him out?

WIDOW – He was four yards away and he was the only one…

DEFENSE – He was on the other side of the street, instead, at least ten yards away! You never recognized the man who shot your husband point blank and you did recognize the other one who was on the other side of the street…

WIDOW – It seemed to me…

DEFENSE – Don't say "it seemed to me!" You must give a sure answer. Is he or isn't he the man?

WIDOW – Before the District Attorney, I recognized him.

DEFENSE – In full daylight, from a yard away! You must recognize him now! And you cannot make a mistake!

WIDOW – I cannot tell now.

DEFENSE – Thank you, Madam!

WIDOW – (*In a very low voice.*) I told the truth…I didn't think…

(*She turns around to look for a moment at the Prosecutor and she quickly moves out. The Defense follows her with his eyes, but he has already begun talking to the Jury.*)

DEFENSE – For everything you will hear in this trial, you must always keep in mind the misery of the human soul. Behold! Inspector Florena's widow would have recognized anyone who had presented himself as the fellow she saw running across the street that night. She was suspected of having her husband killed, she was imprisoned, and ridiculed…but she is only a beautiful woman, somewhat romantic and unhappy who wants to start living again and she needs to show that her husband's murderer is already in the hands of justice. A man comes along…Come forward Rosario Vacirca…sit down…a madman who offers her the opportunity and Florena's widow recognizes him: it's him!

(*He looks at the defendant who is sitting facing the Jury.*)

Honorable members of the Jury, we are in the presence of a profound and mortal tragedy: dozens of men killed, families torn apart, the moral principles of a whole society uprooted, hundreds of people locked up in a cage like animals…and in such a tragedy how far has justice gone? All the evidence has collapsed, not one shred of evidence that can be called certain or infallible. Confessions forced out with violence have been taken back before you. There is not one single witness…The truth of the matter is that in this trial there was only one person who had really seen one of the murderers in the face and could have told us the truth! The mother of the boy Mario Scibilia, killed at the same time as the unionist Alicata…But Concetta Scibilia does not remember anything any more… the pain has driven her nearly insane…Justice therefore holds nothing in its hands…only Giacalone, a little bloodthirsty animal, an illiterate who was brought here by mistake, who killed three men because they beat him, made fun of him and persecuted him…A wretched human being who has nothing to do with this matter, who knows nothing, confessed nothing…The Prosecutor knows all this. That's why he placed all his bets on Rosario Vacirca, the only proof he thinks he has. You have listened to this man: what astonishing lies he has concocted, connecting them one to another! He managed at the last moment, here in the courtroom to involve Filippo Giacalone in his crazy lies…In the pretrial questioning he had never mentioned Giacalone for the simple reason that he had never seen or met him. But during the trial he learned that Giacalone was a driver and knew Luciano Verzì, so he invented that he had fled in Giacalone's car … he said this while Giacalone is ill in the hospital and is not able to call his lie…He invented the last lie, a whole insane concoction without any evidence, without a single confirmation…You heard him… but I want to furnish you with an even more lucid demonstration of his madness and explain the reason for that madness…

(*He turns to the Prosecutor.*)

I ask that all the defendants be brought back into the courtroom, because they have a right to hear…

(*The Prosecutor briefly nods in agreement. A door is opened at the back of the room and the defendants whispering timidly proceed to sit in their places on the benches. They remain silent. The defense attorney has waited unmoving behind defendant Vacirca's shoulders.*)

DEFENSE – All of these men, hunted down, arrested, beaten, kept locked up without food or water, were unable to resist and collapsed at a certain point of their questioning: they confessed atrocious and confused crimes, accusing one another; they invented astonishing crimes...but once they reached the courtroom, before you, they retracted their confessions. Now, I don't know if they are the unfortunate people I think they are, or the murderers that the Prosecution maintains...I simply note this fact, that is, that by denying everything, whether they are innocent or guilty, they have acted according to their instinct of self preservation, which is the most sincere and profound human instinct. That is to say, that they are people who behave in a logical manner, they are reasonable and normal individuals...In their midst, though, there is one who confessed right away and continues to confess. He continuously screams: "I am a murderer! I killed and I saw them kill!" There was no evidence against him, nobody accused him, but he confessed from beginning to end with an obsession that is absurd....It looks like he wants to shape himself into a tragic criminal character...What is the reason for all of this, then?

(*He moves one step closer to the defendant.*)

Listen, Vacirca!

(*He looks at him almost with compassion.*)

Answer the questions I will put to you. Your record was clean...you had never committed a crime...

VACIRCA – No, Sir. Never!

(*The defendant continues to look straight ahead, unmoving. The tone of his voice now is strangely sad, tired.*)

DEFENSE – What kind of work did you do?

VACIRCA – I worked as laborer in the fields or in construction, according to what was available.

DEFENSE – How much did you earn?

VACIRCA – I managed to earn as much as two thousand lire a day. But sometimes I stayed without working for two months.

DEFENSE – Is that why you considered yourself a poor man?

VACIRCA – I felt unhappy.

DEFENSE – What does it mean to be unhappy, for you?

VACIRCA – It means to be miserable. I realized that I was a nobody, I didn't even have any friends...What kind of friends can a laborer have?

DEFENSE – And you had no money?

VACIRCA – Of course not! I never had enough money for the movies, for cigarettes or for a woman…

DEFENSE – For a whore?

(The defendant reacts angrily, but only for a moment.)

VACIRCA – Yes, Sir! Even for a whore! But that is not the only thing…Women don't even look at a laborer…Women know right away how much you're worth in money or substance…If they are whores they want to know if you can pay them and if they are reputable women they want to know how you can support them…All women, more or less, think like whores.

DEFENSE – You were poor, ignorant, despised by women and for this reason you were unhappy… Is this what you meant to say?

VACIRCA – Yes, Sir! That's what I wanted to say. One day I realized one thing…One day, two months before he died, I saw my father who was an old man of seventy-six, crying. He was crying like a baby.

DEFENSE – Why was your father crying?

VACIRCA – Do you know who my father was? Do you know the name he was known by? They called him "Earthworm," which is the lowest form of life on earth. My father was a shit, he was not worth anything in society… He was an illiterate, couldn't read or write, he never knew or understood what was happening in the world, he did not know what the government was. When he saw the town's Police Chief passing by he'd say: "The Government is passing." He spent his whole life in the fields like an animal. Then he had a stroke that left his back and legs paralyzed. He sat in front of his house the whole day and flies walked on his face. He didn't even have the strength to shoo them away. His whole life people had walked on his face and he never had the courage to rebel…He'd reached the point that even if he wanted to kill himself he would not have had the strength to do it… His only vice was tobacco. He needed a pack of smoking tobacco which cost a hundred lire a day. That was the only vice he had….One evening he started crying in desperation…. For his entire life he had endured, but a month before his death, he started crying out of desperation….

DEFENSE – What had happened?

VACIRCA – He had smoked all the tobacco he had. He wanted another pack and I refused to buy it for him.

DEFENSE – And what did you understand at that moment? Your father was a miserable man because he had never earned enough money? Was that what you were thinking?

VACIRCA – I thought that a man cannot live like an animal. There are men who resign themselves and they do it because they are cowards. Money alone is not enough in life…

DEFENSE – What else does one need?

VACIRCA – honor! Having all you need without ever having to beg for charity: a steady job, money in your pocket, feeling like you're somebody in life, I mean, having ten or twenty men like you who consider you a friend and are willing to do anything for you, walking in the middle of the street and knowing that nobody can impose his will on you! I can't explain it well because I don't know the words, but for me this is honor…

DEFENSE – And did your father have honor?

VACIRCA – No, he never did…

DEFENSE –Now listen carefully to what I am asking you, Rosario Vacirca… Did you love your father?

(*The defendant does not answer.*)

I mean to say, did you feel devotion for him, respect?

VACIRCA – No. I despised him.

DEFENSE – Because he was poor, ignorant, resigned, stupid?

(*The defendant remains silent.*)

Go on, answer me!

(*The defendant remains silent. The Defense insists.*)

You must answer me! Tell everyone here why your father spent seven years in jail…

VACIRCA – (*Loudly, shaken.*) All this has nothing to do with the trial…

DEFENSE – (*Continuing, raising his voice gradually.*) And your sister died of illness in an insane asylum…

VACIRCA – (*With a scream.*) This has nothing to do with the trial, nothing to do with it…You can't bring these family matters and discuss them here….

DEFENSE – (*Shouting very loudly.*) You hated your father because he had committed a horrible crime…I have here the judicial dossier and if you want I will read it to you word for word… When you were twelve years old, your father sexually abused one of your sisters, thirteen years old. This was the thing that made you feel miserable… You wanted to forget your family's shame…

VACIRCA – (*Breathlessly.*) I did not want to be like my father, neither ignorant nor poor, like an animal…

DEFENSE – You are not a hoodlum because you were afraid of being poor. You were not poor…you were insane!

VACIRCA – (*Shouting*) I was poor, I was poor…my father was poor…

(*Deep silence*)

PROSECUTOR– Rosario Vacirca, you may return to your seat!

(*The defendant starts out slowly, but the Defense attorney's voice stops him*)

DEFENSE – Rosario Vacirca! Everything you said is false. You are only a little, miserable, compulsive liar who could not even manage being a real hoodlum and simply imagined that you were one… I feel pity for you, because you are really unhappy, but I will wipe you off the face of the earth, I will stop you from dragging other men who are not guilty into your unhappiness…

(*Rosario Vacirca returns to his seat.*)

PROSECUTOR– (*In a loud voice.*) Rosario Vacirca!

(*The defendant is still standing.*)

Do you confess that you killed Carmelo Licitra?

VACIRCA – Yes, Sir.

PROSECUTOR–Do you confirm that you learned that Luciano Verzì had killed union organizer Venero Alicata?

VACIRCA – Yes, Sir.

PROSECUTOR– That you saw Luciano Verzì kill Chief Inspector Ettore Florena?

VACIRCA – Yes, Sir.

PROSECUTOR– And that you learned that the murder had been committed under orders from Emanuele Crupi?

VACIRCA – Yes, Sir.

(*The defendant sits down. There is a moment of silence, almost a lull. Everyone is immobile. Down on the right the black silhouette of a woman has appeared, walking slowly almost touching the wall at the back of the court then she moves forward and sits before the Jury. She is still young, her lips are colorless, her eyes sunken.*)

PROSECUTOR– This woman is Concetta Scibilia, the mother of the boy who was killed together with the union organizer Venero Alicata… She is very ill. Let me explain now the reason for her presence in this Courtroom.. But before I do that I have to relate the events that took place on the evening when the double murder was committed…

(the woman remains immobile without saying a word.)

The Scibilia family lived in a small apartment on a split level building along Crispi Street, in the suburbs. The father was a business man and that night was not at home. The boy was sitting by the window reading; his mother was sitting close by and had stopped reading the papers a few seconds before. She was tired. The radio was broadcasting a program of popular music …It was exactly 7:25 PM, October 18. It was drizzling out and the street was deserted. It seemed there was nobody around…no human voices or footsteps were heard, only five gun shots and the noise of broken glass. The boy was hit by a bullet almost at the corner of his eye and fell to the ground, killed instantly, almost at his mother's feet, as shown in the picture shot shortly afterwards by the *Carabinieri* forensic squad…

(The picture of the boy lying on his back is projected against the back wall. It's focused on his face.)

His mother tried to lift him up with her hand but she saw it covered with blood and realized the boy was dead. Exactly at that moment, her memory fell into darkness. For this reason she has not been able to tell us what happened afterwards. We can only guess this since the boy's body was found exactly where he fell and the woman was found instead unconscious on the landing of the balcony with her face covered with blood, past the pieces of glass that she had broken with her body. At the moment she saw her boy dead, she probably hurled herself against the window to see who had fired the shot. One thing she must have seen for sure…

(In the back, the picture of a human body seen from above, stretched out on the cobble stones with legs spread wide, his jacket opened and a bloody chest.)

Down there, on the cobblestones, lying on his back the dead body of Venero Alicata, killed with three bullets to the chest and one to the face…But we don't know if she was able to make out the face of the murderer. It's certain, however, absolutely certain, that he was still there, at the corner of the street where he had fired from, because only four or five seconds had passed, and he must have looked up when he heard the noise of the breaking glass. There was a moment in which the woman perhaps saw the man's face clearly. That was the man who had murdered her boy!

(The woman lets out an almost inaudible lament, then she shrinks into herself, but her look remains emotionless and immobile.)

PROSECUTOR– Concetta Scibilia, however, has no memory of that moment, the most shattering of her life. Her conscious mind has buried it inside of her...For the instinctive fear of the suffering that the memory would cause her, her mind refuses to remember it. It places itself beyond her will. It's a sort of blind defense of the human being. Scientists compare it to the phenomenon of the fatally wounded animal that tries to hide its wound any way it can in the delusion that death will be kept at bay. Concetta Scibilia has not been able to recall what she saw right after the murders in any of the face to face confrontations...

(*He is silent for a moment.*)

Now, however, we possess a new element: that's why we called Concetta Scibilia into the Courtroom. We've identified the musical piece the radio broadcast the night of October 18 at 7:25 PM. We want to reenact the confrontation here in the Courtroom with the person who is accused of the double murders.

DEFENSE – This is absurd! It's a cruel experiment that has no rational basis for it. The witness has already undergone two confrontations under rigorous scientific controls and did not recall any details. I object. This cruelty is useless!

PROSECUTOR– Only the witness can refuse, if she wants.

(*He is looking at the woman who remains immobile. He nods and Luciano Verzì slowly leaves the cage and goes to stand at the poorly lit corner of the courtroom to the right. From the opposite side slowly enters a middle aged man holding a guitar. He has an attentive face but ordinary. He bows to the Judge who nods in the direction of the bench on the left. Everything is happening as if already rehearsed.*)

MAN– (*In a barely audible voice.*) Yes, Sir!

(*He sits down quickly, placing the guitar on his legs and turning to face the Prosecutor.*)

PROSECUTOR– Mrs. Scibilia, you must try to think only about what happened. You have inside your conscience the image of the murderer. You must free yourself! You can identify the person who murdered your son. Now everything will happen exactly as it did on that evening...

(*In the back the picture of a boy appears.*)

You must be very strong, Mrs. Scibilia. Look at this picture of your boy!

(*The woman remains immobile.*)

It's the picture that you yourself gave us...

(*The woman turns around a looks for a moment at the projected picture without moving. She slowly resumes her position as before. At the same time, the man begins to play the guitar very softly: a sad, endearing tune.*)

PROSECUTOR– Mrs. Scibilia, do you recognize him?

(*Time moves slowly. The Prosecutor insists.*)

Mrs. Scibilia, you saw the man who killed your boy…Tell us if it's him!

(*Concetta Scibilia does not answer. She begins to shake, she takes her eyes off him. Suddenly Rosalia Alicata's scream is heard from the back of the room where she is seated.*)

ROSALIA – Concetta Scibilia, tear his eyes out! That is your son's murderer!… You must recognize him!

PROSECUTOR– Rosalia Alicata, keep quiet!

ROSALIA – (*With the same voice.*) But don't you see his face? Don't you feel disgust for him inside your guts…How can you not understand that he is the man who killed your son?

PROSECUTOR– Rosalia Alicata, that's enough! Please sit down!

ROSALIA – But what kind of man are you, Mr. Prosecutor, sitting there with your black robe, representing justice, and then you stop people from telling the truth?

PROSECUTOR– Officer, escort her to that bench!

(*Rosalia Alicata moves back two steps and resumes her seat. She stops moving. The light goes out and all three move away at the same time, each in a different direction: Luciano Verzì toward the cage, the man with the guitar bows lightly and withdraws quickly and Concetta Scibilia toward the bench at the back.*)

DEFENSE – Madam, You have not been threatened in any way, have you?

(*The woman stops but she does not turn around to look at him.*)

DEFENSE –Madam, did you recognize him as the man who killed your son?

(*She looks at him now, as if she did not understand the meaning of the question. She cannot speak, but her teeth begin to chatter out of a sort of disgust, an unbearable chill. She vacillates. Quickly a Carabiniere holds her up and compassionately escorts her away. At the same time Rosalia Alicata moves forward screaming…*)

ROSALIA – She is afraid…She is afraid. Can't you see she is afraid? That man…He is the murderer! What other proof do you need? He boasted to the whore that he had killed my son…Rosario Vacirca saw him kill with his own eyes…

DEFENSE – Go away, Rosalia Alicata!

ROSALIA – (*Advancing some more.*) Everyone who comes here is afraid... Haven't you heard what they said...didn't you hear the speeches at my son's funeral? The same men who had had him killed! Is this is what you call humanity? It's play acting...Did you look into their eyes? Are these men? They are clowns from the first to the last...the policemen who denounced my son when he was alive...the politicians who followed his funeral cortege...the lawyers paid to prove falsehoods...Counsel, you know these men are murderers and you are trying every trick in the book to show the contrary.

DEFENSE – (*Shouting*) This is an insult to the role of justice!

PROSECUTOR – (*Shouting at the same time*) Rosalia Alicata...

(*But Rosalia's invective against the defendants overpowers their voices.*)

ROSALIA – They are all murderers! They are the bosses in your homes, they pull your strings like puppets...you don't even realize it... they are taking your dignity away from you...

PROSECUTOR – Call the guards!

(*But his voice is overpowered by Rosalia's shout as she moves toward the Jury.*)

ROSALIA – Members of the Jury, don't you have any mercy? You are all there dressed in your Sunday best, representing justice...you look like the Almighty...but out of this room, what are you? Hiding deep inside your dens like mice. People are persecuted and die on the face of the earth and what do you do?... My son...

(*The Carabiniere takes her by the arm from the back, but Rosalia pulls away from him violently, shouting...*)

You must let me speak...My son was murdered because he had rebelled... He was fighting for you as well, but he was alone...My son was stretched out on the street with his jacket torn and his chest covered with blood...and I refused to understand that he was dead...my son had died forever... they didn't even let me touch him, I just wanted to wash his eyes and his mouth... they even pulled me by the hair as they dragged me away... So then, how much is the life of a man worth in this town?

(*Suddenly she throws her head back and she breaks into a tragic and inarticulate sobbing. A long and uninterrupted cry of sorrow and desperation. She allows the Carabiniere to lead her toward the back. Her terrible scream is heard as she moves away then the closing of a door. Silence.*)

DEFENSE – The interrogations period is over. It's almost evening...

(The carabiniere reenters, stops at attention before the Prosecutor, handing him a sheet of paper. The Prosecutor reads it. Silence.)

PROSECUTOR – *(In a loud voice.)* Defendant Filippo Giacalone, alias "Little Christ," who had been in the prison infirmary for three days, has been found in the latrine, dying…

(Absolute silence in the room.)

PROSECUTOR – Giacalone stabbed himself with an old knife blade, once in his throat and once to the heart. According to the first medical report it happened four hours ago and he was found bleeding to death almost …

(Absolute silence.)

None of the prisoners in the infirmary answered the call for blood donors… does anyone among the defendants want to volunteer?

(Absolute silence.)

Defendant Barresi!

(The defendant stands up hesitantly.)

BARRESI – Mr. Prosecutor, I'm a sick man.

PROSECUTOR – I want to ask you something else. You were the last one to talk to defendant Giacalone the night before he was transferred to the infirmary…

BARRESI – I didn't say anything to him… I asked him to lend me his comb, but he refused. I did not even know him. I have already said so…I saw him a few times during exercise time, but before the trial I did not even know he existed…

PROSECUTOR – And you don't know anything else?

BARRESI – No, Sir.

(He waits a moment, then he proceeds to sit down.)

PROSECUTOR – Defendant Luciano Verzì.

(Defendant Verzì stands up.)

VERZÌ – *(He hesitates a bit.)* Mr. Prosecutor, Giacalone was sick. He was always suffering. At night he screamed in pain. He was in very poor health.

PROSECUTOR – One day Giacalone told the Court that you had threatened to kill him…

VERZÌ – It's a lie, Mr. Prosecutor! Giacalone hated me because I had denounced him…Once in prison I offered him a cigarette, but he threw it in my face. Since then I haven't spoken with him…

(*He too waits a moment, then he sits down.*)

PROSECUTOR – Defendant Emanuele Crupi!

(*He answers calmly remaining seated.*)

CRUPI – He tried to commit suicide because he was afraid.
PROSECUTOR – (*Slowly, firmly.*) Stand up when you address the Court!

(*Defendant Crupi stands up.*)

CRUPI – Yes, Sir. That is my duty.
PROSECUTOR– Do you know why Giacalone tried to kill himself?
CRUPI – Yes, Sir. You know it, too, Mr. Prosecutor. He was afraid that they would kill his children. He didn't have any choice. He was afraid that one day or the next they would have forced him to confess: Giacalone, in fact, really knew who had killed the eight policemen. They had told him to steal a car and to drive it to a precise address. He did not know, however, that in the trunk they had wired a load of dynamite and when the tire went flat, he abandoned the car in the middle of the street…that is the truth, Mr. Prosecutor…

(*He gets off the bench and advances by two steps, resting on his cane.*)

The truth is that Giacalone, this miserable, little man who, according to the District Attorney, had an innate criminal vocation, had never killed anyone in reality, and this is something you knew as well, Mr. Prosecutor. You tried to save him from life imprisonment throughout this trial. All you wanted from him in the end were the names of the murderers, to give you the final proof. Giacalone was, in fact, the only one who could have provided the definitive proof. And he understood that … That's why he tried to kill himself.
PROSECUTOR– Defendant Crupi, you are challenging justice!
CRUPI – God forbid, your Honor! I only want to defend Giacalone as he is dying… Everything that had to be said in this trial has been said and justice will do now what it must… I can no longer offend it in any way, nor help it…

(*He moves forward a few steps.*)

Of course, if I were the invincible Mafia boss that you say I am, perhaps I could even tell you all the names of the men I had killed and why…I could tell you the names of the Deputies to whom I gave the votes I controlled and what they guaranteed me in return...I could explain why certain public works were built in an area where it serves no purpose, rather than in another place where it would have assured jobs for two thousand families...for example, why certain dams were not built. They spent billions. If built, the dams would have irrigated thousands of barren acres of land, but they will never be built... I could tell you the reasons for all these things, show them on a blackboard, draw for you the entire cobweb of men who must be connected with one another for a masterpiece of this kind...if I were the Mafia boss you say I am...

(He turns toward the defendants' cage.)

I could list the names of those who were killed and point out with my finger the men who killed them...

(Steps before the cage, looking at all the defendants in the face.)

...call them by name, one by one, and furnish you with the proof. I could do it, if I were the great Mafia boss you say I am, nor would I be afraid to do it because nobody can touch me any more...My heart is dangling from a spider's spit. All it needs is a push to make it fall...nor would I feel shame or remorse, because I have never felt shame or remorse for anything I have ever done...Everyone must have pride in life and he must do things because he believes in them, for the pride.

(He returns slowly toward the Jury.)

The only thing is that I feel weak, exhausted... The moment has arrived even for me when a man begins to have compassion for other human beings and sees things as they really are...

(He sits before the Jury, looking before him and he will not turn his head to look elsewhere for the rest of his speech.)

...but if I were the great Mafia boss you say I am, without fear by now or reserves or retractions, I would not tell you any way because in life everyone must play his part until the end. You are the ones who must do justice...I am not on the side of justice. I maintain that justice is made by men of our time and is, therefore, imperfect, stupid, and corrupt...this, too, I could show and tell you what you need to corrupt a judge, what you must give him in exchange...

PROSECUTOR – Mr. Crupi, you are an old lawyer with the privilege of speaking in your own defense, but you continue to insult justice with impunity.

CRUPI – If that is so, I sincerely beg your pardon, Your Honor. I have no intention of insulting your person…You want justice, it's your duty, and I respect you, but this is not true justice. The truly important things happen outside this courtroom and you, Mr. Prosecutor, will never have the possibility of modifying them…Even if Giacalone stays alive and you manage to establish his innocence, what purpose would it serve? He will continue to be poor and afflicted by what you called his criminal vocation, a wretched illiterate. Do you call this justice?

PROSECUTOR – (*In a loud and firm voice.*) Defendant Crupi, I forbid you to continue insulting this Court!

CRUPI – (*Protesting.*) If what you say is true, you could not stop me from killing twelve men and now you want to stop me from speaking… How can you? What can you do to me? Charge me with contempt of Court? I stand accused of twelve murders and you want to charge me with contempt?

(*He has difficulty catching his breath. He places his hand before his eyes for a moment, then he resumes looking straight ahead.*)

Forgive me! I don't know if it's my eyes that are growing dimmer, but perhaps it is getting dark, night is really falling…

PROSECUTOR – Defendant Crupi, is this a confession you are making?

CRUPI – Confession of what? If you have no evidence? In reality, everything happening in this trial does not concern me any more. I am a dead man…I feel death on me like a suit and it fits me well and comfortably. I understand now what union organizer Alicata must have felt each time he went home from one of his furious speeches in defense of the peasants. He knew he was carrying death on him and he wore it well, like a beautiful suit…You see, Mr. Prosecutor, that was a real man. I take my hat off to him because he had dignity and honor, he had understood that a man must fight from beginning to end…but men like him are few and justice cannot defend them…

(*The light at the back of the courtroom has been growing imperceptibly dimmer for a few minutes. Suddenly the desperate and tragic scream of Rosalia Alicata reverberates and dies out. At the back, in the falling shadows, the carabiniere appears. He makes two steps forward and remains at attention. He nods affirmatively. He will not move from that position until he is totally enveloped by darkness.*)

PROSECUTOR – Giacalone is dead!

(*A brief and general mumbling among the defendants.*)

CRUPI – You shouldn't feel too badly. He just saved his children's lives.

PROSECUTOR – It's as if you murdered him. You forced him to commit suicide!

CRUPI – Wrong, Mr. Prosecutor! Giacalone died as was proper for him! Nearly all men who lack courage are forced at a certain point in life to accept their fate… The truth is that most men are afraid, they're willing to suffer the greatest humiliation to avoid taking risks… but can't you see how men let themselves to be killed in war? Their whole life they think it will never happen to them to die like that and they don't rebel, they seek refuge in their cowardly hope…

PROSECUTOR – This is a trial and we will condemn the murderers…

CRUPI – Yes, Sir! The trial is over and now you are called upon to issue a verdict. Perhaps, you will sentence these men accused of murder, but everything will remain as before since behind them in this world there are countless other wretched human beings, and if you leave this Courtroom you will find hundreds of them willing to kill for a million lire, and others who for ten or twenty thousand votes are willing to exploit the stupidity and ignorance of the poor…an endless number of other cowardly men…

(Darkness has continued to fall over the Courtroom, swallowing by now everyone, except the defendant facing the Jury.)

You too are afraid. Every day you endure terrible things happening around you… Corruption, poverty, human beings abandoned to violence… What are you willing to sacrifice yourselves for? Should they kill your children before your eyes…

(Everything is in the dark. Only a small, luminous spot illuminates the defendant and, at the back, the picture of the murdered union organizer.)

But on the day when your turn comes, you won't be able to run away any more, nor will your voice be loud enough for someone to come and save you…

(For the third time, out of the darkness, that tragic, endless woman's scream, as the curtain falls.)

MARQUIS

Marquis imprimeur inc.

Québec, Canada
2007